WHAT PEOPLE ARE

THAT OPTION NO

Because of the radical directions and possibilities opened up by the left of the 1970s the period has since been demonised by media, corporate and political establishments alike. And yet retrieving the real history and ideas born in the experimental turmoil of those years is vital for breaking out of the present era of reaction. In *That Option No Longer Exists* John Medhurst has done the left a huge service by carrying out exactly this retrieval and doing it with rigour and flair. A really excellent book.
Hilary Wainwright, Director Transnational Institute, Editor Red Pepper, Author of *Beyond the Fragments* and *Labour: A Tale of Two Parties*

John Medhurst has produced a brilliantly written polemic, with real verve and style, on leftwing politics and policies in the Britain of the 1970s. He demonstrates how the left of the Labour Party had both cogent analysis and viable policies to move the country forward but was undermined by right-wing colleagues, the media, and the entire panoply of the secret state apparatus.

The book redefines the 1970s and will be widely read as a contribution to the current debate on the future of the Labour Party and the labour movement.
Roger Seifert, Professor of Industrial Relations, University of Wolverhampton Business School, author of *Revolutionary Communist at Work: A political biography of Bert Ramelson*

John Medhurst offers an important and well-informed account of the state of the UK during the early and mid-1970s, and a new perspective on the Wilson and Callaghan governments of the mid to late 70s. The analysis challenges the prevailing mainstream view of this period as one dominated only by crisis and instability and offers a more positive interpretation. As such the book presents a long overdue alternative perspective on the period before the advent of the Thatcher era, particularly when it comes to the role of the trade unions and broader left. Medhurst presents a thorough analysis of the internal and external challenges the Labour governments in Britain faced during that period. This book is highly recommended for anyone interested in British political history. It will hopefully contribute to a new perspective on Britain under Labour in the 1970s.

Dr Christian Schweiger, Professor of Government and International Affairs, Durham University, author of *Britain, Germany and the Future of the European Union*

In *That Option No Longer Exists*, John Medhurst provides a lucid and powerfully argued case for returning to the middle years of the 1970s to understand what social, economic and political progress could have been made in Britain. He shows that these years were a turning point, with the potential for progress stymied by the forces of right-wing conservativism and reaction. Critically, he suggests that we have in our power the ability to re-imagine that sort of potential today.

Gregor Gall, Professor of Industrial Relations, University of Bradford, author of *Tommy Sheridan: From Hero to Zero?* and *An Agency of Their Own? Sex Worker Union Organising*

That Option No Longer Exists

Britain 1974-76

That Option No Longer Exists

Britain 1974-76

John Medhurst

zero
books

Winchester, UK
Washington, USA

First published by Zero Books, 2014
Zero Books is an imprint of John Hunt Publishing Ltd., Laurel House, Station Approach,
Alresford, Hants, SO24 9JH, UK
office1@jhpbooks.net
www.johnhuntpublishing.com
www.zero-books.net

For distributor details and how to order please visit the 'Ordering' section on our website.

Text copyright: John Medhurst 2013

ISBN: 978 1 78279 600 8

A CIP catalogue record for this book is available from the British Library.

Design: Lee Nash

Printed in the USA by Edwards Brothers Malloy

We operate a distinctive and ethical publishing philosophy in all
areas of our business, from our global network of authors to
production and worldwide distribution.

CONTENTS

To Sue, Elizabeth and Eleanor

Acknowledgments

I would like to thank a few people who kindly offered me special advice and assistance in preparing this book and related material for publication, without whom it would not have seen the light of day in its present form:

Hilary Wainwright, editor of *Red Pepper* and author of outstanding books on socialism from the 1970s to today, for her participation in launching the Brighton Peoples' Assembly in 2013 and her encouragement and help with the manuscript; Gregor Gall, Professor of Industrial Relations at the University of Bradford and Editor of the Scottish Left Review Press, for his invaluable advice on key parts of the book and other kind assistance; Roger Seifert, Professor of Industrial Relations at the University of Wolverhampton Business School, for a critique of an earlier draft which improved the final version and his subsequent positive comments (especially generous as he does not agree with some of my interpretation); Dr Christian Schweiger, Lecturer in the School of Government and International Affairs, Durham University, and principal co-ordinator of the University Association of Contemporary European Studies (UACES) research network on Europe and the financial crisis, for valuable input on the EU and for facilitating my involvement in UACES policy seminars in Brussels, London and at Cambridge University; Davy Jones, the outstanding Green Party Parliamentary Candidate for Brighton Kemptown, for passing on a vital request for assistance and ensuring it was answered; Carolyn Jones, Director of the Institute of Employment Rights, for letting me blog on their website; and Tariq Goddard, for his help and welcome at Zero Books.

Also thanks to colleagues past and present within the British and European Trade Union Movement. In my three decades as a member, elected representative and employee of the civil service trade unions CPSA and PCS I have known many activists and officials at all levels who helped me along and kept the faith in dark times. I could not list them all but I offer a special salute to Amanda Millhouse, Julie Wyeth, John Khan, Tom Taylor, Martin John, Chris Hurley, John Baldock, Stuart Roberts, Susan Garcia, Terry Adams, Charlie Cochrane, Nadja Salson, Enrico Tortolano, Denis Lenihan, John McInally, Sue Bond, Chris Haswell, Pam Cole, Norina O'Hare, Natasha Burgess and Paul Bemrose.

Lastly, as the opportunity may not arise again, I would like to pay tribute to some personal political inspirations – the artist, designer and eco-socialist William Morris; the most outstanding Labour politician of the 20th century Aneurin Bevan; the Marxist historian and radical humanist E.P Thompson; the epic truth teller and libertarian socialist Noam Chomsky; the courageous campaigner for secularism and human rights Peter Tatchell; the "Leader of the Opposition" Green MP Caroline Lucas; and, of course, Tony Benn.

John Medhurst
Brighton & Hove – March 2014

We reject the Bolshevik way of posing the question – victory first, reform after – because the absence of reforms makes for defeat and not for victory. But we also reject your way of putting it – reforms first and a revolutionary assault on counter revolution after – because it may happen that nothing survives to be reformed if counter revolution gains a decisive victory .

Julius Martov, Leader of the Russian Mensheviks, 1919

Do the British people really want a society in which industrialists and bankers have more power over Britain's economic future than the governments they elect?

Tony Benn, 1973

Introduction

History for the losers

The 1970s in Britain are once again a source of intense political controversy and debate. A core theme of the *Daily Mail*'s attack in September 2013 on the politics of Ed Miliband's father, Marxist academic Ralph Miliband, was that the son wished to return the country to the "nightmare Seventies".[1] Whilst the *Mail* supplied some perfunctory and shallow references to what it was that made the 1970s a nightmare – for example, the standard-for-the-time Price Control Commissions that were "like something from a Soviet tractor co-operative" – the attack had little to do with Marxism as a system of thought or even with Ralph Miliband himself; it was merely a useful means to attack Labour's belated adoption of mild social democratic economic policies such as a short term freeze on soaring energy prices. Similarly, a criticism by the Chief Economist of the Institute of Directors on Labour's proposal to compel large developers to use rather than hoard land was paraphrased by the *Mail* as claiming the policy was similar to "Stalin's notorious seizure of land from prosperous Russians".

Likewise the Murdoch press has always been consistent with its spin on the 1970s, especially the so-called "Winter of Discontent" in which, according to the *Sun*'s Political Editor Trevor Kavanagh, the Labour government and the trade unions supposedly took Britain "to the edge of economic meltdown".[2] In reality the strikes of that period inconvenienced relatively few, and compared to genuine catastrophes like the collapse of UK manufacturing in the 1980s or the banking crisis of 2008, had little economic impact. Despite this, the legend of the Winter of Discontent is now virtually cast iron, impervious even to the admission of Derek Jameson, editor of the *Daily Express* in 1979, that "We pulled every dirty trick in the book. We made it look like it was general, universal and eternal, whereas it was in reality scattered, here and there, and no great problem".[3] Because of these constructed myths there is now almost universal agreement in mainstream media and historiography that the 1970s were indeed a nightmare decade, a pressure cooker of extreme politics and economic decline, a build up of social dysfunction that required Margaret Thatcher's harsh monetarist medicine to purge and clean.

This unreflective and ill informed view of the 1970s was canonised as official dogma after the death of Thatcher in April 2013. Although there were routine references to how "divisive" a figure she was (there had to be some reason that much of the north, Scotland and Wales virtually celebrated her passing) there was little or no deviation from the standard line that she had come to power at a time of national crisis and decline, and had in an admittedly stern and uncompromising manner reversed that decline and dragged the country towards a more sustainable future. As a reconstruction of a period and its historical significance this is essentially propaganda, manufactured and repeated even more often than those other potent fictions: that Labour Prime Minister Jim Callaghan said "Crisis, what crisis?" in response to strikes in 1979, and that Michael Foot wore a donkey jacket to the cenotaph during his time as Labour leader. Neither is true, yet most media commentators repeat them as if they are, and they have entered the nation's collective historical memory.

It is now a heresy to maintain that the economic situation Thatcher inherited in 1979 was not quite as grim as later history would have it. Inflation was heading down and North Sea oil was coming on stream. The 1974-79 Labour government had been particularly unlucky in that its time in office coincided with the capital investment phase of North Sea Oil exploration rather than with the results and profits of that investment. Its Tory successor reaped the benefits and then squandered them, using North Sea Oil revenues to fund tax cuts for the middle class and paying benefits to more than three million unemployed instead of using it, as Labour intended, as the basis for national economic recovery. It was a criminal waste of a natural asset, as the Thatcher governments used the money "to manufacture a consumer boom which directly benefited British consumers, Japanese exporters, foreign wine interests and the Dordogne tourist industry".[4]

Even with the shield of North Sea Oil, Thatcher's record on the economy over the course of the 1980s was essentially a failure. Nor is this a retrospective insight. In 1981 the UK Treasury Committee on Monetary Policy, with a seven to five Conservative majority amongst the MPs who sat on it, conducted a major examination of monetary policy, specifically the empirical justification for monetarist economic theory as expounded by the neo-liberal economist Milton Friedman. After taking evidence from Freidman himself as well as critics of monetarism such as the Keynesian economist Nicholas Kaldor and considering all extant economic data and case studies, the Committee concluded that there was no proven connection between the money supply and inflation, or with the level of public spending. The Committee found that increase in the money supply was not due to government spending but to bank credit, which the Heath government had freed from regulation and the Thatcher government had no intention of reversing. The final conclusion of the Committee was that monetarist economic theory, the basis for the entire Thatcher revolution, was "theoretically unsound and practically inoperative".[5]

Thatcher's solutions to the economic "malaise" of the 1970s were not a series of tough choices demanded by tough times. They were political prejudices dressed up as sound economic doctrine. As has been pointed out on the margins of political comment, she failed on the economy "not just in terms of the huge social costs – the trashed lives, the forsaken communities, the needless destruction – but also on her own terms".[6] Inflation was higher when she left office than we she entered it, and the effect of mass unemployment on British society was devastating, fuelling riots and despair, as whole regions of the country were left to a meltdown that did not concern the right-wing media except as an excuse for sterner policing measures. From the first years of her first government, Thatcher applied an extreme economic dogma that had the immediate effect of "plunging the country into the sharpest, deepest recession since the war to that time"[7], which it did not begin to emerge from until 1988. For most of the 1980s growth was exactly the same as the 1970s and on a par with average growth rates in other western European countries of the time. Thatcher's unimpressive economic record, intimately connected to her ideological agenda to crush organised labour and de-regulate finance capital, was delivered in tandem with a slew of reactionary social policies like Clause 28. This is now almost a hidden history.

Yet in some economic commentary the real history, or at least a factually sound and valid interpretation of it, can still be found. An analysis by Alan Bailey, Under-Secretary for industrial policy in the Treasury 1973-79, of the 1974-79 Labour government's industrial policies, finds that Labour's attempt at a "systematic industrial strategy" had more to recommend it than is ever accepted in "the prevailing caricature of the period".[8] Bailey notes correctly that whilst the 1974 Labour manifestos talked rhetorically about taking charge of the commanding heights of the economy, the actual concept of planning agreements co-ordinated through a National Enterprise Board (NEB) was focused on the need for cooperative longer-term planning at sectoral and firm level, and was based on a successful French model whereby individual firms were persuaded to commit to investment and job creation in exchange for public grants or purchasing.

The approach had something in common with German and Japanese corporatism. It could hardly be called socialist, let alone

Marxist, except by the unusually virulent and hysterical British right. Tony Benn – and his political advisers such as Stuart Holland and Francis Cripps as well as, outside government, Ken Coates of the Institute for Workers' Control – did attempt to link planning agreements to an enhanced role for trade unions within industry, and devolve strategic decision making to workers through their unions. This was highly contested in theory and practice. In theory because it was always more likely that the unions' National Executive Committees and full time officials would dominate these interactions rather than plant level workers; and in practice because British business through the Confederation of British Industry (CBI) was adamantly against any involvement in strategic and investment decisions by its own workers, at any level or in any manner.

Bailey concedes that it was difficult to secure the necessary information in order to effectively target strategic investment, and admits that without a realistic budget and a firm mandate to impose planning agreements the National Enterprise Board ended up saving and protecting only "lame ducks" – although most economists give little consideration to the positive impact on local economies and quality of life of providing training and employment in otherwise deprived regions. Nevertheless the attempt at an activist industrial policy was beginning to bear fruit by 1979 and its broad lineaments such as better knowledge in Whitehall of British industry's long term needs and more effective regional strategies are now, in 2014, being revived in a belated attempt to reverse the decline of British manufacturing.

None of this has prevented the right-wing media feeding the myth of Margaret Thatcher's "success" in comparison to the "failures" of the 1970s. Simon Jenkins, a not unintelligent commentator on many subjects, went so far as to claim that "Britain in the 1960s and 1970s was, in European terms, a failed state".[9] This is a ludicrous assertion given that the UK was a perfectly functional constitutional democracy during this time (indeed, in "Swinging London" it had one of the most influential and vibrant urban centres of Europe) that entered the EEC in 1973 and immediately became one of its major players. The one truly dysfunctional part of the UK in the late 1960s and 1970s, Northern Ireland, which was stripped of civil liberties and local democracy and subject to covert military operations, is not criticised by Jenkins as such. Such myopia on the right is standard but many icons of the liberal middle-class commentariat also endorse and repeat these fictions, giving them a credibility and acceptance they would lack were they confined solely to the right-wing press.

The BBC has an especially poor record in this regard. Its coverage of Thatcher's death, funeral and legacy was notable for its lack of balance, automatically assuming that her political significance denoted positive achievements of a usually unspecified kind. This should not have been a shock given that the BBC's prestigious History webpage, used by many British schools for basic introductions to key events and people in British history, has a capsule description of Thatcher in its Prime Ministers and Politics Timeline that begins "Britain's first female prime minister came to power with the country descending into industrial and economic chaos", and concludes that even though she still divides opinion, "Nonetheless, she is generally considered to be one of the best peace time prime ministers of the 20th century".[10] That such a positive assessment is deeply controversial and would probably be contested by a majority of British people makes it all the more inappropriate and partisan.

The website hammers its theme home with its brief description of Thatcher's predecessor, Labour Prime Minister James Callaghan. With no reference to any other events in his three year premiership after taking over from Harold Wilson in 1976, the website describes Britain as "strikebound" with "food and fuel supplies undelivered, rubbish uncollected, and – most notoriously – bodies unburied" (this of two instances in

Liverpool and London where due to industrial action some bodies were kept on ice – everywhere else in the country the dead were buried as normal). The writer then loses any semblance of balance at all, adding that "Things became so bad in Hull that it was dubbed 'the second Stalingrad'".[11] This is a reference to the fact that, for a few weeks, Hull's central co-ordinating strike committee had overseen and controlled delivery of the fuel and food that the website claims in the previous sentence was left undelivered, something which prompted Philip Larkin to write to his friend Kingsley Amis of his hatred for the "lower class bastards" who had taken over the city.[12]

Similarly, when the BBC's Chief Political Correspondent Andrew Marr made and presented a major five part history of post war Britain, the episode on the 1970s briefly mentioned that Labour under Harold Wilson was elected in 1974, and then jumped straight to the "Winter of Discontent" in late 1978/early 1979, the uncollected rubbish on the streets and the unburied dead. There were no references to Labour's 1974 manifesto commitments, or Tony Benn's efforts to introduce a radical Industry Act, or the "Social Contract", or the IMF crisis of 1976.[13] In official BBC history the Labour government of 1974-79 had one theme and one terminus only – massive strike action that led to the election of Margaret Thatcher.

Yet there is another story, seldom reproduced by BBC History notes. A comprehensive survey by Professor Danny Dorling of the share of the nation's wealth retained by the richest 1% of the population between 1918 and 2012 found that that share had been falling since 1923 (the election of the first Labour government) and was at its absolute lowest in 1974-76.[14] From 1979 that trend began to reverse itself, so that in 2014 the share of the nation's wealth owned by the top 1% is once again back at 1918 levels and heading towards Victorian levels of inequality (this figure itself conceals a much bigger and unprecedented level of wealth inequality, in that the lower range of the top 1% can earn as little as £120,000 per annum, whilst the top end – about one thousand people – are simply off the scale). The High Pay Commission's Final Report on pay inequality (2011) found that pay for top executives in many FTSE 100 companies increased by an average of 4,000% in the last thirty years. Amongst others the report cited the pay of former Barclays chief executive John Varley who the report said earned £4,365,636 – 169 times more than the average worker in Britain.[15] This equates to an increase of 4,899% since 1980 when the top pay at Barclays was £87,323 and only 13 times the UK average. Clearly British society and the UK economy turned a significant corner in 1979, but the direction it then took was away from a flawed but functional social democratic welfare state with healthy social outcomes and towards greater poverty and wealth inequality.

Unfortunately for those who seek to present the 1970s as a grey decade of decline and defeat, its social and cultural reality stands as a living rebuke, so much so that even the *Financial Times* conceded that it is time to re-examine "the glamorous and playful 1970s",[16] a belated recognition that the era of Laura Ashley, Biba and Roxy Music could not forever be dismissed as dour and tasteless. Much depends, of course, on perspective.[17] The surge of industrial militancy from 1970 to 1974 that propelled a radicalised Labour Party into power may have disheartened financial and business leaders, but it was exhilarating and liberatory for the far larger number of people who took part in it. Squats, rent strikes and communes expanded the horizons of many and challenged fixed social hierarchies. Women began to exercise and enjoy more social and sexual freedoms than ever before. A vibrant and glamorous music scene lit up the downtime and Saturday nights of working class youth. Nor do surveys of the views of the ordinary people who lived through the 1970s support the "consensus" of contemporary middle-class commentators. On the contrary they demonstrate the exact opposite. A comprehensive survey by the New Economics Foundation – based on social inequality, investment in public services, levels of pay and other benefits to ordinary workers – found that 1976 was by all indicators the "happiest year" in the period 1945 to date.[18] No survey has ever found this to be true of any of the Thatcher or Blair years, and it is a certainty that no one will ever claim it of any year in the second decade of the 21st century.

For most commentators this is counter-intuitive and embarrassing. If they cannot ignore it they must therefore discredit it. A review of Dominic Sandbrook's *Seasons in the Sun* – a classic of conservative anti-70s hyperbole – by Chris Snowdon of the free market think tank the Institute of Economic Affairs, is not simply effusive praise for Sandbrook's sour and extremely biased portrayal of the period 1974-79 as "bleak, bizarre and tragicomic", but a forceful dismissal of inconvenient evidence to the contrary.[19] It targets the New Economics Foundation's survey specifically and warns that there is "a danger of the Seventies being re-imagined by the losers". It approves Sandbrook's dismissal of the NEF's findings about the 1970s as based on "a strange index" because, after all, "the diaries and letters of those who lived through it are soaked in the darkest pessimism", ignoring the reality that only a sliver of middle and upper class people will have written and kept letters and diaries, and that this evidence is therefore too unrepresentative a sample to be used as a general picture of the times.

Beyond ignoring and marginalising survey findings that undermine the misrepresentation of the reality of life in the mid 1970s, it is of course the *politics* of the period – specifically the socialist challenge presented by a resurgent Labour left and trade union movement, and a wider range of radical social and cultural movements – that right-wing commentators wish to caricature, diminish and deride. To do that, a massive and almost monolithic re-writing of history must take place, and it has. The attacks on the 1970s from both right-wing and supposedly liberal commentators are a glimpse, rarely accorded us, of the fear and outrage of an otherwise comfortable possessing class towards lower orders who get above themselves. The aim of this short book, therefore, is to reinstate the 1970s – and specifically the early to middle years of the decade – as one of the most politically fertile, liberating and exciting periods in British history, and to focus on 1974-76 as the crucible of a struggle within government now almost forgotten.

As will be clear from the content and length, it is not an academic or a comprehensive work. Nor would I make any claim to originality except in the selection and presentation of relevant material. The focus is inevitably political although it touches on social and cultural issues to reinforce and add context to the main argument. It is a history consciously and deliberately "re-imagined by the losers" and as such it is closer, I would argue, to what actually happened.

Chapter One

The Big Flame

The British Labour Party was elected to office in February 1974 on the most radical reforming programme in its history. Explicitly socialist, it exceeded even "Let us Face the Future", Labour's 1945 General Election manifesto, in its ambition to challenge and control the citadels of private wealth and power. The programme laid out in the manifesto was extensive. It committed to taking North Sea oil and gas reserves into full public ownership, as it "cannot accept that the allocation of available world output should continue to be made by multi-national companies and not by governments". It also announced its firm intention to take shipbuilding, ship repairing, the manufacture of airframes and aero engines, marine engineering and the ports into public ownership and control, as well as sections of pharmaceuticals, road haulage, machine tools, and construction. It would do so as an essential element in a wider strategic programme whereby the government would "take over profitable sections or individual firms in those industries where a public holding is essential to enable Government to control prices, stimulate investment, encourage exports, create employment, protect workers and consumers from irresponsible multi-national companies, and to plan the national economy in the national interest".[1]

The reasoning and justification for this programme was made very clear. It was to effect "a fundamental and irreversible shift in the balance of wealth and power in favour of working people and their families", in pursuit of which a Labour government would introduce strict price controls on key services and commodities, return to local authorities the power to fix rents "which do not make a profit out of their tenants", fund a massive extension of social housing, and introduce an annual wealth tax on the rich including a new tax for major transfers of personal wealth. It would also "heavily tax speculation in property". Labour's vision of radical reform extended to more than just redistributive legislation and state direction of industry. It explicitly aimed to democratise existing nationalised industries, working with the trade unions to make the management of these industries "more responsible to the workers in the industry and more responsive to their consumers needs". Yet within two years, despite some genuine progressive reforms, very little of this ambition remained and the International Monetary Fund (IMF) was instructing the Labour' government's Chancellor, Denis Healey, on the direction of economic policy and the exact level of public spending cuts it considered necessary.

Labour's political radicalisation in the early 1970s was driven by two things. Firstly, massive disappointment with the 1964-66 and 1966-70 Labour governments, which had attempted little substantial reform of the economic and political structures of contemporary Britain, with the notable exception of liberalising laws on censorship, homosexuality and abortion. That these reforms could be introduced by a right-wing social democrat Home Secretary, Roy Jenkins, speaks volumes. They were certainly welcome and liberating new social freedoms but it is arguable that their time had come and they did not unduly challenge or discomfort the securely established power elite of Great Britain. What did discomfort it was the renewed determination of trade union and Labour Party members, after bitter disillusionment with the governments of the 1960s, to ensure that next time the party would enter office with sound and unambiguous socialist policies. Thus no sooner was Labour in opposition than the 1970 party conference adopted a resolution put to it by the National Union of Public Employees (NUPE) to create a programme "to secure greater equality in the distribution of wealth and income" as well as "extend social ownership and control industry and land by socialist planning". Another motion, passed against the wishes of the party's National Executive, "deplored the Parliamentary Party's refusal to act on Conference decisions"[2] and set in motion a campaign to ensure that in future it would be more answerable to Labour Party members. This was the starting pistol for a process of policy reformulation that culminated in Labour's Programme for Britain 1973, which Michael Foot called "the finest socialist programme I have seen in my lifetime".[3]

The other driver of internal radicalisation was the 1970-74 Conservative government's political and legal assault on the trade unions. From its election in 1970 the Heath government attacked public sector trade unions in particular. The legislative crux of its attack was the Industrial Relations Act, which demanded that all unions "register" under the Act and only then receive legal immunity from prosecution for breach of contract when taking industrial action. The terms of a legal trade dispute would also be heavily circumscribed and it would be illegal to take any form of secondary or solidarity action. In the context of the time this was seen by the entire trade union movement as an intolerable restriction of trade union and civic rights, a class-based attack on the freedom of action of workers which left employers and big business as unregulated as ever. Impelled by new, more militant leadership in the big unions, the TUC's response was uncharacteristically uncompromising – it declared a policy of non-cooperation with the Act and a major national campaign against it.

The British labour movement, even the traditionally more pragmatic trade unions, had always possessed a core of politically conscious militants. Most of these were based in or around the Communist Party, and from 1968 its trade union operating lever the Liaison Committee for the Defence of Trade Unions (LCDTU). The LCDTU became a prime mover in left politics in the late 1960s and early 1970s thanks to the CPs intelligent and respected Industrial Organiser Bert Ramelson and his skilful promotion of the CP's "Broad Left" strategy, whereby CP and other left union officials formed alliances to advance policy and attain positions within the unions.[4] As a result, CP and CP-friendly officials such as the young Arthur Scargill were elected to sit on many unions' National Executive Committees (NECs) giving the CP an influence within the trade union movement vastly out of proportion to its numbers.

The wave of political radicalism that jolted British society in the 1970s was driven by more than just the CP's Broad Left strategy or the outcome of internal union elections. It arose especially from the disconnect between the emancipatory cultural movements of the 1960s and the hardening economic crises of the 1970s. The 1960s had seen the first stirring of "identity politics" – the self-conscious coalescence of hitherto marginalised sectors of British society (women, gays, ethnic minorities) in to organisational groupings to proclaim and advance their interests. In the early 1970s, ground breaking and influential groups such as the Gay Liberation Front and the National Women's Liberation Movement began to campaign publicly and their activities started to break up a social status quo that had hardly shifted since 1945. This found expression at all levels of contemporary art and culture, from the fine arts to the popular. The cultural commentator Stewart Bradshaw, writing in 1981 as the legacy of the previous decade was coming under severe political and ideological attack, found that in the 1970s there was "a lack of centre in contemporary art" which he saw as a reflection of a deeper loss of centre in the wider society, in that "in the seventies the optimism, faith in the future, and the belief in a mainstream largely disappeared". Whilst the dissolution of a mainstream in the 1970s is certainly true, what that mainstream was and whether vibrant contemporary art required a stable centre in order for it to flourish is debatable. In complete contrast, other critics have found that it was the very breakup of the mainstream that fired artistic experimentation, and have suggested that "what was new and significant about art in Britain in the 1970s was its repoliticisation and feminisation, its attempt to connect to society at large".[5]

That politicisation extended to the timbre and events of everyday life. There was a growing radicalisation of attitudes as a strain of collectivist working class politics began to enter and influence iconic centres of British culture.[6] This went far beyond the acceptance of overtly working class actors and photographers like Michael Caine, Terence Stamp and David Bailey. For a decade from the mid 1960s to mid 1970s the tabloid *Daily Mirror* adopted under its combative editor-in-chief Hugh Cudlipp a genuinely radical edge and a confrontational attitude to many totems of the British establishment. The relaxation of state censorship of books and films underpinned this, but equally important to the subversive culture of the 1970s was the unprecedented opening of BBC TV drama to socialist and working class writers such as Jim Allen and Trevor Griffiths and directors like Ken Loach (whose *Cathy Come Home*, in 1966, had already established him as a filmmaker who could translate radical politics into emotive drama).

Allen especially exemplified the trend. An ex-miner and union activist who had taken up professional writing, his work was explicitly political. After a few years of sneaking political issues into the popular soap *Coronation Street*, he addressed them directly in his TV play *The Big Flame* (The Wednesday Play, BBC, 1969) which followed the progress of a dockers strike. *The Rank and File* (Play for Today, BBC, 1971) presented a dramatised account of the spontaneous wildcat strike in 1970 at the Pilkington Glass factory in St Helen's, Lancashire. It told the story of the unofficial strike committee that emerged to lead the action and flayed the full time union officials who left its members to be victimised after the strike was over. *The Rank and File* was directed by Ken Loach, with whom Allen later wrote and produced the epic four part historical drama series *Days of Hope* (BBC, 1975) about working class life from the First World War to the 1926 General Strike from the perspective of trade unionists and their families.

The best of these televised political dramas eschewed the narrative pitfalls of Marxist agit-prop for an indignant, emotive anarcho-syndicalism. They reflected the emergence in the late 1960s and early 1970s of non-hierarchical organisations campaigning outside the usual political structures, propelled initially by the example of the broad based and popular Vietnam Solidarity Campaign (VSC). During the 1970s these groups grew beyond their middle class roots, as working class campaigners began to assert their rights and demands in fields such as health and housing. Housing policy had always touched working class people, literally, at home – many of them lived in sub-standard private or social housing. Labour's great post-war social housing building programme under Housing Minister Aneurin Bevan had initially aimed to provide quality homes with space and privacy.[7] But this intention was quickly swamped by subsequent Conservative governments seeking merely to meet targets regardless of quality and, even more disastrously, the large scale destruction of terraced housing in favour of high rise blocks and soulless estates, the largest of which degenerated into high crime areas.

With this massive, if misguided, expansion of council houses there was little regulation of the private and rented sector, and the Heath government was not minded to introduce any. Its policy on housing was entirely regressive and was brutally expressed in the 1972 Housing Finance Act. The Act mandated increased "Fair Rents" for most Council houses and phased out government subsidies to local authorities for their upkeep, requiring them to make a profit on the housing stock. It twisted the knife further with a provision that if Councils did not demonstrate how they were implementing the Act they would be denied all subsidies and individual Councillors would be surcharged and debarred from office. As private rents rose steeply in the early 1970s, and the effects of the Housing Finance Act were felt by Council tenants, there was a massive counter reaction. Rent strikes led by the National Association of Tenants and Residents occurred in Glasgow, Liverpool, Sheffield, Southampton, and London. These sometimes grew beyond the confines of the NATR or local trade unions, as in Kirkby, Liverpool, where women from the "Big Flame" Marxist group organised together with women on the Tower Hill estate to form the Unfair Rents Action Group and run a rent strike from October 1972 to December 1973.[8] Self-organised tenants and squatters rights campaigns also began to focus on the quality and amount of the social housing stock as well. If not driven by trade unions or left activists this could have mixed and ambiguous results, as "The shifting political climate meant that protests were being heard from various groups, some of which belonged to the political left or centre, some of which belonged to the right (especially those demanding the right-to-buy in the early 1970s), and many of which were not interested in traditional politics but simply wanted a decent home and service".[9]

Many cities experienced a huge increase in organised and politically conscious squatting of empty properties. By 1974-75 nearly 50,000 people across the country were squatting in abandoned public and private properties.[10] London was inevitably a focus for this activity with an estimated 30,000 squatters and whole streets taken over in Elgin Avenue and Tolmers Square. The Family Squatters Advisory Service (FSAS) offered legal advice and its more militant wing the All London Squatters (ALS) advocated direct action and a more explicitly socialist agenda. Hackney especially developed a visible squatters movement based on the borough's high numbers of homeless people and many empty Council properties, with squatting sometimes organised out of the Centreprise radical bookshop and workers' co-operative in Dalston Lane. In 1973 squatters invaded Hackney Town Hall to protest evictions and homelessness and in 1974 the movement began to contest eviction from GLC properties in the courts.[11] In affluent Bloomsbury a collection of ex servicemen and women occupied the large and empty Ivanhoe Hotel in 1973 to highlight how homelessness sat side by side with unused property. Nearby, at the junction of Oxford Street and Tottenham Court Road, the thirty-three floor skyscraper Centrepoint had increased in value from £5million to about £50million since its construction in 1963 despite remaining unoccupied all that time. In 1974 it was invaded and occupied by housing activists as a symbolic protest.

Tolmers Square, off Euston Rd in Camden, was a circle of Georgian terraced houses which had been unoccupied for twenty six years despite a chronic need for new homes in the area. Due to be demolished for new office development in the early 1970s, the entire Square was squatted and turned into a commune by an alliance of local residents and conservation activists. The back garden walls were knocked down for communal allotments and other houses were converted to a community centre, a bookshop, a health food shop and a free school. The reorganised gardens were implicitly political, "a challenge to private property and atomised domestic arrangements".[12] This was often a conscious ideological stance. During the 1970s many land and property reclamation projects of this type drew upon the example of British communitarian movements of the 17th century such as the Diggers.[13] In this way one subversive counterculture reached out across the centuries to another. The Tolmers Square experiment survived for six years, a beacon of vibrant communal living in the heart of London. Although it was small and transient it did more than simply ask for more resources from local council or government. It took them, and built something different.

Others seeking to break through the social and institutional barriers of post-war British society, such as feminist artists whose challenge to established gender roles and privileges often left them "excluded from the existing gallery and patronage systems", could sometimes find allies in progressive local government. In April 1973 five female artists persuaded Camden Council to let them exhibit their art ("Exhibition on Womanpower") in the recently built Swiss Cottage Library, a modernistic behemoth designed by Sir Basil Spence. The 90 paintings and posters displayed were therefore seen by a wider cross section of people than would have been the case in a West End gallery. The exhibits were deliberately militant and provocative. Some of the images had stencilled slogans across them demanding "Wages for Housework" and "Abortion, a woman's right to choose"; printed manifestos attacking male power and privilege "aroused intense interest and extreme reactions both for and against".[14]

John A. Walker's work on radical art in the 1970s reveals a significant expansion of community arts activities, whilst conceding they were of variable quality. What was most positive of the trend was "a strong desire on the part of many artists to escape from the isolation of the studio, the existing gallery system and its middle-class audience" in order to reach and affect working class audiences. Some of this was no doubt patronising and unsuccessful but at its best it provided people excluded through poor education and regional inequality a way to experience art in their lives, whether it be radical poetry reading, street theatre or political history murals. Bringing art to the masses was one part of a spreading and highly visible counterculture that emerged in London and other British cities at the beginning of the 1970s. The alternative culture of the 1960s – a mixture of drugs, hippie fashion, radical psychology and revolutionary posturing epitomised by the 1967 Dialectics of Liberation congress at the Round House in London's Chalk Farm – had in all essentials been confined to a small middle class elite. In the 1970s the dam broke and "the seventies counterculture was in comparison a sprawling shambolic mass of activists and fellow travellers, all busily hacking away at the oppressive structures of mainstream society".[15]

The strands of this culture meshed and cross fertilised, most especially in a network of communal living experiments and squats that took over some of the derelict houses of then unfashionable inner city areas like Woodstock Road in Birmingham, Cheltenham Road in Bristol, Moss Side and Victoria Park in Manchester, and whole areas of Hackney, Islington, Brixton and Clapham in London. Some of these were centres of Marxist and feminist agitation and were genuine attempts to live outside a commercialised capitalist value system. Many had little choice but to do that because of sheer lack of funds and eventually fizzled out as people got older and local councils started to re-possess. But in its heyday, in the opinion of an outsider fleeing the German police for her activities in the Red Army Faction who fetched up in a commune in Hackney, "the alternative sub culture in seventies London exceeded, in size and diversity, what had emerged in other Western cities. Women's and gay rights groups, food co-ops, the Poster Collective, All London Squatters, film collectives, underground magazines".[16]

A particularly visible and subversive part of this alternative sub-culture was the "Free Festival" movement which took off in 1972. The first Free Festival, organised on a shoestring and a printing press from a South London commune, was held illegally in Windsor Great Park as an explicit anti-monarchist statement, and was promoted as "Rent Strike: The People's Free Festival". It grew in numbers in the following years until it was brutally attacked and dispersed by the police in 1974. After this it became the Stonehenge Free Festival which ran from 1974 to 1984 although its initial core of political anarchism was gradually swamped by a wave of New Age Travellers. The Free Festival movement has since transformed into a mainstream cultural jolly for the young middle-class but it was born out of a challenging radical ideology which has left a permanent impact. Many of the themes and issues that are a staple of the British progressive left today – uncensored artistic expression, the promotion of non-corporate local produce, alternative festivals, ecological activism, sexual equality – had their genesis in the cultural underground of the early to mid 1970s.

The personal was also political, sometimes in the most intimate fashion. The surprise bestseller of 1972 was Alex Comfort's *The Joy of Sex*, which sought to educate and illustrate in a positive, uninhibited and non-judgmental manner the varieties of (heterosexual) sexual experience. Comfort, a life-long anarchist, had written for the anarchist journal *Freedom* in the 1940s and 1950s and was a member of the CND offshoot "Committee of 100"; he was arrested in Trafalgar Square with Bertrand Russell in 1961 for non violent direct action. By the 1970s Comfort's main work was in biology but his anarchism provided a moral and political basis for what was called "Sexology" (he hated the term). He made that clear in his 1973 book *More Joy of Sex*, arguing that "The anti-sexualism of author-itarian societies and the people who run them doesn't spring from conviction (they themselves have sex) but from the vague perception that freedom here might lead to a liking for freedom elsewhere". Perhaps pushing his argument too far, he claimed that "People who have erotized their experience of themselves and the world are, on the one hand, inconveniently unwarlike and on the other violently combative in resisting goons, political salesmen and racists...".[17]

The large social base of the trade union movement – its 13 million members and their friends and families – lived amongst and to a degree absorbed these multiple challenges to estab-lished institutions and values. Although only ever a minority, an increasing number of young union activists in the early 1970s were rediscovering and reading Marx, Lenin and Trotsky, and following the activities of Tariq Ali and other left-wing campaigners in the UK. Some even spent time in "revolutionary" left parties such as the International Socialists (IS) and the International Marxist Group (IMG). They sympathised and identified with the Vietcong and Salvador Allende in Chile, and read about their struggles in publications such as *Socialist Worker*, *Black Dwarf*, *Big Flame* and *Socialist Challenge*. Many drew their analysis of the Labour Party's failings from Ralph Miliband's *Parliamentary Socialism* and their deep suspicion of the British State from the same author's *The State and Capitalism*.[18]

Nor was this wave of militancy solely a male affair. The 1970s had began with the passage of the Equal Pay Act (propelled into being by the strike action of female machinists at the huge Ford Dagenham plant, at which they received less pay than men for the same work) although employers had five years to adjust to its provisions before it came into effect in 1975. The first National Women's Liberation Movement conference took place in February 1970, giving the "women's movement" a shape and a focus. The following year the NWLM adopted its Four Demands which were for equal pay, equal educational and job opportunities, free contraception and abortion on demand, and free 24 hour public nurseries. Socialist feminist groups soon formed within the movement and the UK's first explicitly feminist magazine, *Spare Rib*, was launched in 1972. Political activism was important, but equally so, for young working class women entering the workforce and looking for role models, was the expression in popular culture of women's growing independence and self-respect. Whilst the male characters of sitcoms like *On the Buses* or *Steptoe and Son* were either pathetic sexists or tragic failures, the young women of *The Liver Birds*, which ran from 1969 to 1978, were increasingly confident and assertive.

Historic advances in the legal status and protections afforded to women also followed, as issues such as routine spousal abuse were acknowledged and addressed for the first time. In 1971 the first women's refuge centre in the world for female victims of domestic violence, Chiswick Women's Aid, was opened by the feminist campaigner Erin Pizzey. The impact of Pizzey's work led to the formation in 1974 of the National Women's Aid Federation and eventually to significant legislation such as the Domestic Violence and Matrimonial Proceedings Act (1976) which mandated restraining actions against violent husbands, and the Housing Act (1977) which specified that women and children at risk of violence were homeless and thus eligible for benefits and temporary accommodation.

In 1970 women made up 37.7% of the total workforce (in 1979 they would be 41%), and roughly a quarter of those were working part-time. The demographics of work cultures were shifting rapidly but trade unions were not responding with sufficient speed. Many women's working patterns raised issues around homeworking, flexible hours, and child care that unions did not prioritise, perhaps because the internal culture of the unions was still heavily male. By 1976 the proportion of women elected to trade unions' National Executive Committees had risen to an average of 15% but only 7% of their full time officials were women.[20] Not until the 1980s did unions begin to realise the importance of targeted recruitment of the vast part-time and heavily female workforce. Despite and because of this women on the left and inside the trade unions were mobilising. As they did so many looked to new, less hierarchical forms of organisation than they found within the unions and the traditional socialist parties, which were almost without exception run by men whose personal politics rarely precluded patriarchal attitudes to female comrades. Inspired and reinforced by socialist feminists such as Sheila Rowbotham, author of *Women, Resistance and Revolution (1972), Women's Consciousness, Men's World (1973)* and *Hidden from History (1974)*, female trade unionists stretched the definitions and expectations of the labour movement. The Working Women's Charter emerged from the London Trades Council and focused on issues that in later years trade unions would advance as central bargaining objectives: a minimum wage, maternity leave, crèches and nurseries, and equality audits by employers.

The small political parties to the left of Labour had less concrete impact, although sometimes their newspapers, such as the IS's *Socialist Worker*, attained a wider readership. The IS (in 1977 it became the Socialist Workers Party) had been growing in numbers since the late 1960s. The lacklustre record of the Labour government, plus the electrifying effect of May 1968 in France and the Prague Spring, had attracted students and some trade union activists to its confident Trotskyism and its slogan "Neither Washington nor Moscow but International Socialism". In 1971-72 the print order for *Socialist Worker* went up from 13,000 to 28,000 and its readership may have exceeded 50,000.[21] This was mainly because of the high calibre of its writers with contributions from fluent and powerful journalists like David Widgery, Paul Foot and Christopher Hitchens. But as much as readers enjoyed the paper and its contribution to a broader political culture beyond Westminster, the impact of the IS on the organised labour movement was minimal due to fundamental weaknesses of philosophy and tactics.

Politically the IS remained trapped within Leninist dogma, which was useful as a critical cudgel to backsliders but otherwise could not absorb the obvious reality that most of the British working class had always and still did put their faith in a reformist Labour Party and defensive trade unions. This was the "self activity of the working class" that the IS sought in theory but undermined in practice by a rigid democratic centralism and manipulative Vanguardist approach to political campaigning. Its attempts in the early to mid 1970s at creating a network of "Factory Branches" were a complete failure, essentially because the IS seemed to regard modern Britain, in all its social and cultural complexity, as a larger version of war torn 1917 Petrograd. Even if revolutionary politics were relevant or applicable (and a sense of revolutionary *possibility*, most especially the need to defend a radical left government from subversion and military coup d'etat, was certainly necessary) political and insurrectionary strategies suitable for a semi-feudal autocracy simply did not translate to the cities and workforce of 1970s Britain. For all its energy and passion, the IS was not attuned to, or particularly interested in, the real political opportunities that opened at this time as a result of the radicalisation of the Labour Party.

Chapter Two

The Socialist Challenge

That there was social and political turmoil in Britain in the 1970s is incontestable. That some socialists imagined this might open up a revolutionary situation is also true. But for the majority of working class men and women the revolutionary fantasies of small parties like the IS and IMG were simply irrelevant, and the only credible vehicles to advance their interests remained the Labour Party and the trade unions. Despite the failures of Labour and the unions in the 1960s this was a perfectly realistic assessment and a reflection of the strength and appeal of a genuine trade union-Labour Party alliance.

The key figures within a re-invigorated and resurgent trade union movement were Hugh Scanlon, General Secretary of the Amalgamated Union of Engineering Workers (AUEW) since 1968, and Jack Jones, General Secretary of the Transport and General Workers Union (TGWU) since 1969. Both had risen from the shop floor. Scanlon was a member of the Communist Party from 1937 until 1954, utilising his CP contacts to rise in the AUEW from Shop Steward to full time National Organiser. He held this post until he was elected as the "Broad Left" candidate for AUEW General Secretary in 1968. Jones, easily the most respected and influential of the two, had fought in the International Brigades in the Spanish Civil War where he had been wounded. On his return he became a militant TGWU activist in Coventry where amongst other activities he kept war production going throughout and after Nazi carpet bombing of the city.[1] After the war he became the Midlands Regional Secretary of the TGWU before emerging as the left candidate for General Secretary in the late 1960s.

Trade union leaders like Jones and Scanlon were significant

but they could not and did not stand alone. They drew their power and confidence from a labour movement that had rediscovered its class consciousness. The key to the political transformation of the Labour Party from the demoralised rump of Harold Wilson's tired and morally bankrupt government in 1970 to a confident socialist attack force in 1974 lay in the frontal challenge to the Heath government that erupted out of working class communities during those years. Although the great Miners' Strikes of 1972 and 1974 are remembered and used by right and left to define the era, in many ways the wave of worker occupations and sit-ins in the early years of the decade are more representative of a working class that was increasingly confident and innovative in its tactics.

The occupation of Upper Clyde Shipbuilders (UCS) in 1971 lit the touch paper. When a request to the Tory government for a £6 million loan to keep the massive plant going was rejected it set off a chain reaction, fuelled by militant shopfloor representatives and instinctive class solidarity. On 24 June 100,000 workers in Glasgow stopped work in protest and 50,000 marched through the city demanding the shipyard be kept open. The government, used to ignoring Scotland, announced immediate receivership with the loss of at least 6,000 jobs. The effect of this on Scotland's broader economy would have been devastating. Two days later UCS workers led by Communist shop stewards Jimmy Reid and Jimmy Airlie took over the plant, not to strike but to demand "the Right to Work". Reid in particular, who "had the ability to convey trade union demands in terms that invoked ethical values and Christian imperatives",[2] caught exactly the tenor of the UCS militants in a speech to assembled workers broadcast around the world. He told them firmly that "There will be no hooliganism, there will be no vandalism, there will be no bevvying" and urged that to maintain the support of a broad front of people the workers needed to demonstrate self-discipline and firm organisation, not merely a token loud protest. The workers agreed to finish the ships being built and to work with a broad front of politicians and campaigners to find a means to rescue the business. Support for the occupation was so high that in August 200,000 workers across Scotland took further action to show support and over 80,000 people marched in Glasgow. The Chief Constable of Strathclyde Police told the government that if it attempted to evict the workers from UCS he could not guarantee order in the city.

The UCS occupation set the Labour Party alight. A UCS delegation to the 1971 Labour Party Conference received a standing ovation. Tony Benn visited the work-in, offered support and led marches in Glasgow. The Institute for Workers' Control (IWC) drew parallels with the Split shipyards in Yugoslavia which were managed by its workers. Even after a rescue package was agreed (£35 billion to save three of the four yards) the boldness and imagination shown by the UCS work-in set off a wave of occupations across the UK. Between 1972 and 1974 there were over two hundred further factory and plant occupations and sit-ins making a variety of demands to do with employment and conditions. They followed each other with escalating defiance and energy – numerous steel and engineering works in South Yorkshire in late 1971; Sexton, Son and Everhard Shoe Manufacturers in East Anglia in February 1972; Bredbury steel-works near Manchester in early 1972, followed by dozens of engineering plants around the city; Stanmore Engineering in London in late 1972; Briant Colour Printing in East London and Leadgate Engineering in Durham in 1973; and the Meriden plant of NVT motorcycles in late 1973.[3] The spirit and strategy behind these were exemplified by a shop steward at the Fisher Bendix motor components plant at Kirkby on Merseyside (where women from the Fair Rents Action Group were organising against rent increases) who after 200 workers occupied the company boardroom and urged management to reconsider closure plans, told his members "Better we occupy, to control from within, rather than stand out in the rain and the cold, trying to stop scab lorries".[4]

Occupations and sit-ins, sometimes followed by attempts to permanently reject managerial hierarchies and prerogatives and set up workers' co-operatives, were controversial actions on the left. For those who sought a total revolutionary transformation of society they were simply short-term tactics to escalate the temperature and raise class consciousness. For ordinary workers, most of whom did not think in these terms, any action that asserted their rights and started to take back some control of the work process was a step forward. For the socialists of the IWC occupations, sit-ins and co-ops were "encroachments" on capitalist management and the first stage of a continuum of challenges to its power and privileges. It was, they argued, the beginning of a longer process, it "raised questions of alternative futures for the organisation"[5] and should not be dismissed in favour of either complete control by the State or a possible (but in sober reality highly unlikely) future revolution. These were not rarefied debates. The period between the occupation of UCS in 1971 and the Miners' Strike of 1974 was a period of intense political radicalisation, fuelled by the growth within the traditional labour movement of Marxist concepts and analyses usually confined to academic discussion.

Powerful and sophisticated theory was useful but it could achieve little without social and industrial shock troops to bring it to life. Increasingly, it had these. Nothing demonstrated this more vividly than the 1972 Miners' Strike and its dramatic climax at Saltly Gates depot, the last big stockpile of coal left in the country. About 250 lorries a day took coal supplies from the depot. For the strike to succeed it needed to be shut down. NUM pickets at Saltly went from 200 to 1,000, but still most of the lorries were not turned back. The NUM called upon unions based in and around Birmingham to take solidarity action and on 8 February a delegate from the NUM's Yorkshire Executive, the

33 year-old Arthur Scargill, addressed the District Committee of the AUEW. Scargill, at the height of his oratorical powers, carried the meeting and it was agreed that the Committee would organise strikes and a mass picket at Saltly Gates two days later. On 10 February, 50,000 car and engineering workers took strike action and 10,000 marched to Saltly Gates to join the miners' picket. Saltly stayed shut and unions at plants across the region promised that if it re-opened they too would join the picket.[6] After this, and an escalation of power blackouts caused by the dispute, the government retreated and quickly conceded the miners' demand for a 20% increase for coal face workers.

Defiance of the government spread beyond the workplace, driven by local housing activists and left-wing Labour Councillors as much as the big trade unions. At Clay Cross in Derbyshire eleven Labour Councillors, already implementing a radical form of redistributive municipal socialism and freshly inspired by the miners' victory at Saltly Gates, refused to implement the terms of the Housing Finance Act which required them to raise the rent of Council Housing tenants. All the Labour Councillors, including David Skinner, the brother of the ex-miner and socialist Labour MP Dennis Skinner, were surcharged, bankrupted and banned from holding Council office for life. The local community rallied around, leading to large marches and demonstrations in support and a further politicisation of everyday life. Across the country Labour Party activists demanded that a future Labour government reverse the findings and indemnify the Clay Cross councillors.

The centrifugal force of resistance to the government was the challenge of the Industrial Relations Act of 1971. The attempt to force unions to register under the Act was met with massive and co-ordinated resistance. In July 1972 five shop stewards at a container depot in East London were fined by the National Industrial Relations Court for refusing to obey a court order to stop picketing. They were then arrested and imprisoned for breaking the Act. Dockers set up a permanent picket outside Pentonville prison and the "Pentonville Five" became a *cause célèbre* across the trade union movement. Printers offered support and Fleet Street shut down. London bus drivers, porters and lorry drivers joined in. Workers at Heathrow took strike action and closed the airport. The TUC had to respond quickly or lose all credibility with the unions it was supposed to speak for. Preparations for the first General Strike in Britain since 1926 were well advanced when the government once again backed off and conjured up a legal pretext to release the men.[7]

A victorious miners' strike, local Council resistance to central government, a mass movement to secure decent social housing and a threatened General Strike; this was a potent brew, with unpredictable outcomes. Not for nothing have some British socialists called mid 1972 a "Glorious Summer": "All this led to an unparalleled blossoming of democracy. Political discussion and debate, for so long confined to Parliamentary chambers, suddenly became part of the daily life of many thousands of workers".[8] This "blossoming of democracy" even penetrated the internal structures of the Labour Party itself. Key personnel changes saw some of the old Cold War warriors depart and a new cadre of officials, influenced by the radicalism of the late 1960s and early 1970s in which they took part either as students or trade union activists, assume influential positions inside the Party machine.

The appointment of Ron Hayward, an ex-trade union official, as General Secretary of the Party in 1972 opened the gates for this new wave of left-wing officials to join or be promoted. He "altered the ethos of Transport House from the tool of the leadership to that of the servant of the party and this transformation was reflected throughout the organisation".[9] Hayward was contemptuous of moribund party branches run by tribalist hacks with barely a political thought in their heads.[10] His abolition of the Proscribed List, whereby activists with allegiance to a variety of smaller socialist bodies could not be Labour Party members, was endorsed by the 1973 Labour Conference. This re-energised the party by letting in and empowering members who were driven by political principles more than by unquestioning party loyalty regardless of policy.

Labour's "New Left" had learned the lessons of the 1950s and 1960s when glorious Bevanite rhetoric had been outclassed and out-argued by the intellectual analyses of right-wing revisionists such as Hugh Gaitskell and Tony Crosland. This time the left realised that "to win the argument rhetoric had to be replaced by detailed research".[11] The detailed research and policy programmes were not slow in emerging – from a re-energised Labour Party Research Unit led by Terry Pitt, from the IWC, and from the policy work undertaken by Stuart Holland. Holland had cut his teeth in the Cabinet Office and in Harold Wilson's Political Office during the 1966-70 Labour government, but despite Wilson's high regard for him (the PM tried to appoint him Economic Advisor to the Foreign Office but the FCO resisted), he left the government in frustration at its failure to implement Labour's National Plan for the economy. Since 1968 he had taught at Sussex University and had served on the Industrial Policy and Public Sector sub-committees of Labour's NEC.

Holland's most important work, *The Socialist Challenge*, was not published until 1975, a year after Labour had taken office and when many of the internal struggles to implement its key policies were virtually over.[12] But the groundwork had been done in the early 1970s when he presented papers to Labour's NEC that formed the basis of the industrial strategy laid out in Labour's Programme 1973. The core of Holland's philosophy was that the State, in alliance with the trade unions, must take a leading strategic role in the pursuit of socialist economic policies. Based on an analysis that highlighted the power of multi-national companies to shift production across borders and avoid political control, Holland argued for the central role of a National

Enterprise Board (NEB) and Planning Agreements across major industries to give trade unions a key role in strategy and delivery. Holland's "Framework for Bargaining of Planning Agreements and the Social Contract", laid out in his NEC papers and his 1974 policy summary *Strategy for Socialism*, gave union Regional Executives input into major companies' business strategies and put union NECs on a par with government departments in overseeing their implementation.

On one level Holland's analysis was concrete and specific, with detailed schema drawn up by him and the TUC-Labour Party Liaison Committee in 1972/73 for what would be Labour policy for the restructuring and expansion of British industry and for the Planning Agreements to underpin that. These policies, in themselves, were not especially socialist. A version of this kind of state capitalism had been practised in Germany, France and Japan since 1945 with demonstrable economic success. Certainly those countries had outperformed the UK in productivity, investment and the growth of domestic industry. Where Holland left European and Japanese corporatism behind was in his stress on using state and institutional power not simply to control aggregate demand but to ensure a redistribution of power and wealth. Keynesianism, the dominant economic policy paradigm since the Second World War, was above all designed to rationalise capitalist *production*, to ensure that the market would function more efficiently, and that a fairer distribution of rewards would contribute to social stability. Holland acknowledged the importance of the Keynesian multiplier and demand management but in his view it required the socialisation of leading, strategic manufacturing firms to guarantee investment promotion, increased productivity, price control and regional regeneration. Unlike Labour's social democrats, based around Tony Crosland, Holland emphasised that only through the public management of *supply* would greater social justice, wealth redistribution and economic democracy be achieved and maintained.

Having served in the 1964-70 Labour governments, he had seen first hand how bold plans for the leading role of the new Department of Economic Affairs (DEA) had been quickly subverted by market led deflation and immediate political retreat, so much so that by 1969 the DEA officially acknowledged that "what happens in industry is not under the control of the government".[13] Like Tony Benn at the Ministry of Technology, another new Ministry set up to exploit and direct Wilson's "white heat of technology", Holland conceded that "Labour's National Plan started in a statistician's dream world but ended in a nightmare of deflation".[14] Unlike those on the social-democratic right of the party, Holland and Benn did not want to simply repeat the experience of 1964-70 and hope for better luck next time. Benn made this clear at Labour's 1973 conference. "The crisis we inherit when we come to power," he told delegates, "will be the occasion for fundamental change and not the excuse for postponing it".[15] Citing the rise of multi-national companies and the challenge of international financial markets now freed from exchange rate control, he argued for public ownership of the UK's leading firms as an essential democratic check and a vital resource in the armoury of elected governments to determine economic policy in line with their manifesto commitments. He referenced the creative and successful interventions of the Italian Istituto per la Ricostruzione Industriale (IRI) in investing in impoverished regions, through taking controlling shareholdings in major Italian companies and placing them within a planning framework. Even Roy Jenkins, for a time, was swept along with the new thinking and fresh policy coming from Holland and the Home Policy Committee. In 1972 he made a speech praising the IRI as an example of what a British state holding company directing strategic investment could achieve.[16]

This analysis fed directly in to the 1974 General Election Manifesto, which laid out guidelines for selective public ownership to "harness the power of the big private companies in the public interest". The proposal, derived from Labour's Programme 1973, was that the transition to greater public ownership would be overseen by the NEB which would initially base itself on existing state shareholdings but with "a substantial addition of some twenty five of our largest manufacturing companies". This was never intended as a rigid target but it became the basis of what a hostile media routinely described as "the top 25 companies". The issue blew up not solely because the media attacked it but because Wilson made clear that he did not support the policy. He was quite willing to make a rhetorical commitment at the October 1973 Conference to a further expansion of public ownership because he knew that once in office Labour's Cabinet, in which right-wing social democrats would hold the majority, would not follow through on it. He therefore made a public statement that whilst the NEC had the right to put its agreed policy programme to the Conference, the policy contained in the next Manifesto would be decided jointly by the NEC and the Parliamentary Committee (the Shadow Cabinet) who "would not hesitate to exercise its veto at the appropriate time".[17]

In a sense the exact number did not matter. It had been chosen by the Home Policy Committee and the NEC to tie what they knew was a reluctant leadership to a specific programme of public ownership that would give a Labour government strategic direction of the "commanding heights" of the economy. It was all a step too far for Labour's major players, including Jones and Scanlon who wished to concentrate on immediate issues of wealth redistribution through changes to pensions and taxation, as well as safeguard the legal position of the unions. Neither was Michael Foot, whose socialism had always been light on economics, particularly interested in specific nationalisation proposals. In the end Labour's ultimate fixers, the Conference Arrangements Committee, organised matters so that the

Conference Motion supporting nationalisation of the top 25 companies was "composited" with a Motion proposed by supporters of the Trotsykist Militant Tendency to nationalise the top 250 monopolies. This motion would obviously be rejected as too extreme, as it was, and so the lesser proposal on the top 25 companies and the solid anchor it would have provided the NEB and the wider industrial strategy also fell.[18]

It was a clever manoeuvre by Wilson and a portent of the future, but the core of the policy still remained. The criteria for which companies would be taken into public ownership was clear – the likely effect of doing so on job creation in areas of high unemployment, a proven need for investment promotion and technological development, growth of exports and import substitution, and their usefulness as a counter weight to the dominance of private multi-national companies in the UK. These criteria influenced Labour's 1974 White Paper *The Regeneration of British Industry* and the 1975 Industry Act introduced by then Industry Secretary Tony Benn, although by 1975 the already defunct "top 25" would be reduced almost to zero and much of the Planning Agreements that would have held them together as part of a national strategy would be voluntary. Although this would neuter and disarm Labour's policy to force British industry and the City to think and act strategically, the 1973 Programme held other, perhaps even more subversive challenges to the industrial status quo. For the first time since the great "Labour Unrest" of 1910-14, a movement for grass roots workers control within industry had arisen to discomfort both employers and trade union bureaucrats alike.

Chapter Three

Workers' Control

Labour's "left turn" was not simply an academic exercise led by Stuart Holland. His work was the policy reflection of a subterranean current in the broader labour movement, a profound questioning of an entire corpus of political and economic assumptions barely challenged (except by precursors of monetarism like Enoch Powell and Keith Joseph) since 1945. Long before Margaret Thatcher attacked the perceived failings of nationalised industries, a movement for grassroots industrial democracy centred on the Institute for Worker's Control (IWC) had brought these issues to the fore. The IWC was a breath of fresh air in the Labour Party, a much-needed injection of libertarian thinking into its tired Fabian orthodoxies. Holland's bold and original economic policy work supplied the intellectual rigor to buttress it. And the trade unions were restless, looking to use their power to advance working-class interests as they saw them. But all these disparate elements needed to be pulled together. Above all they needed a focus, an enabler and a political leader.

The leader was Tony Benn. In the 1950s and early 1960s Benn was a keen young technocrat personally closer to Hugh Gaitskell than Nye Bevan, but he had been radicalised by his struggle to renounce his unwanted inherited peerage (which prevented him sitting in the House of Commons), by his experiences in the 1964-70 government, and by the influx of Marxist ideas into the wider labour movement in the early 1970s. Never a Marxist himself he was nonetheless a principled democratic socialist who drew personal inspiration from a very British tradition of radicalism from the Levellers to the Chartists to the syndicalists. Although condescended to by social democrats such as Tony Crosland and Denis Healey, at the height of his political influence during the

1970s and early 1980s Benn displayed far more powerful conceptual thinking and strategic vision than his right-wing colleagues. Above all he understood the tectonic shifts in the Labour Party, which Wilson, Callaghan, Healey and Foot – all in their different ways mired in the politics of the 1950s – found baffling. He looked forward, not back.

It was this quality which he brought to his Chairmanship of the Labour Party in 1971-72. His becoming Chair at that time – there was no real contest, it was essentially "his turn" – opened floodgates that could not easily be closed. A seminal analysis of Labour policy making concedes "The year of his chairmanship was the year that the real foundations for Labour's policy was laid down".[1] Benn was an activist Chair who visited local party and trade union conferences arguing for a fundamental re-examination of party policy. To that end, his 1971 paper *Towards a Socialist Industrial Policy* floated the idea that a future Labour Government would introduce an Industry Act that would give the government powers to buy shares and assets in, and make loans to, any company it wished to direct and run. Later attacked as authoritarian, Benn actually eschewed the use of conventional nationalisation and sought methods to intervene that were quicker, more flexible and democratic (i.e that reflected the input of the employees as well, regardless of trade union structures). His paper argued that government money could "...help declining industries, finance advanced industries," and should be utilised so as to "expand the public sector and create a public portfolio and central management unit that would profoundly shift the balance of power in favour of the public sector".[2]

Benn never saw this as helping "lame ducks"; indeed it was explicitly never meant to be so. He envisaged the creation of a new sector of the economy run to and through criteria other than profit for a small number of shareholders. It was this thinking that brought him to the IWC. Founded in 1968 to encourage ideas and schemes for greater industrial democracy in British industry and shop floor control of the production process, the IWC was a challenge not just to the CBI and established management hierarchies within private industry but also to the managers of the state owned industries and the full time officials of the trade unions with whom they often worked in tandem. In investigating grassroots industrial democracy Benn was doing the exact opposite of seeking to please the trade union "pay masters" of right-wing demonology.

This was new territory for Labour. Despite its nominal commitment to "the common ownership of the means of production, distribution and exchange" Labour's policy planners had hardly thought through the mechanics of such a programme and the extent to which public ownership opened up the possibility of decentralised industrial democracy within those bodies – i.e. handing strategic direction and management to the workers themselves. The 1945-51 Labour government had nationalised the mines, the railways, civil aviation, the electricity, water and gas industries (and the Bank of England, although it had left its powerful Court and relations with the City unreformed). The new nationalised industries were certainly more accountable and were forced to consider the wider social and employment consequences of their operations, but "the government was deeply suspicious of anything remotely "syndicalist" that might provide more grassroots or shop floor representation and influence on the Councils of the nationalised industries".[3] Its conception of socialist planning was entirely top down and corporatist, with a few "safe" trade union leaders (usually fierce anti-communist bureaucrats who spent much of their time crushing leftist trouble makers within their unions and preparing for eventual elevation to the House of Lords) ensconced on the Boards of nationalised industries, where they seldom questioned the financial advice of the full time management. Inevitably, the nationalised industries were deeply compromised. On the one hand they were used to provide private industry with a subsidy in the form of cheap services and infrastructure and to maintain employment in regions where the private sector failed to take off, and on the other, their London based Boards remained distant from their workers and vulnerable to criticism for not performing like unencumbered private firms with no wider public responsibilities.

The IWC was the first organised labour movement grouping to challenge the role and structure of the nationalised industries as fundamentally undemocratic and to examine power relations within both public and private industry. It brought together trade union militants, shop stewards and socialist theorists under one umbrella and with an increasingly popular goal. It was led by Ken Coates, who, in the opinion of the historian Eric Hobsbawm (writing in the *New Statesman* in 1973), was "the most under-rated political analyst among British Marxists today".[4] Coates was a former Communist who had left the CP in protest at Stalin's attack on Tito's Yugoslavia and who went on to help form and lead the Bertrand Russell Peace Foundation. He now espoused a mixture of libertarian socialism and localism, specifically how to devolve decision making power in industry to the workers within each concern. He was also one of the few Marxists of the period to break with a growth-oriented model of economic development that promoted industrial expansion regardless of its wider long-term effect on the natural environment. His essays on the subject, collected in *Socialism and the Environment* (1972) dared to suggest that the left could and should encompass ecological concerns as part of a programme of anti-capitalism and responsible social justice.

In some respects the IWC's ideas were a reflection of the variety of workers' self-management introduced in Yugoslavia from 1950. An ambitious attempt to break away from the centralised State Socialism of the Soviet bloc, in the Yugoslavian model the direction of regional economies was delegated to semi-autonomous republics with central government departments running "co-ordination councils" to integrate economic production on the national level. Elected Workers' Councils at regional and plant level controlled production and most of the profits were distributed among workers, not the state or an elite of owners and shareholders. Whilst the government assisted with industrial and infrastructure development there was a genuine level of industrial democracy and workers control, consistent with the wider socialist goals of the economy and the society. Coates and other IWC contributors referenced the Yugoslavian experiment as a form of decentralised participatory socialism that, though by no means perfect and overly dominated by the Communist Party, was worth studying.

Benn found Coates to be congenial political company, and his ideas influenced some of his policies when Benn became Industry Secretary in 1974. Benn was open about this and admitted that Labour's policy-making process had drawn much from the UCS occupation and from the ideas about workers control that had emerged from it. In his *Arguments for Socialism* (in which, from the perspective of the early 1980s, he looked back on lessons learnt in the 1970s) he admitted that "This was the first step beyond the corporatist idea of public ownership planned from the top". He attributed the new thinking to events on the shop floor and concluded that "if those events had not occurred when they did and in what form they did, the Labour Manifesto of 1974 would not have reflected any aspirations beyond the traditional Morrisonian approach to public ownership".[5] Coates had moved far from that traditional approach. In his 1973 essay "Socialists and the Labour Party", he claimed that "Tenants associations, residents committees, bodies airing and voicing the complaints of whole populations on council estates, in ghettoes and slums...Claimants unions which attempt to organise people living on social security, the unemployed, and strikers claiming benefit" were examples of groups that needed a firm political voice, and that this voice should be a radicalised Labour Party.[6] He viewed this as a democratic socialist variant of Trotsky's "transitional programme" and he was unafraid to draw the parallel – "Trotsky saw the need for a social programme of immediate demands which led out of one social order into another, and about this need he was certainly profoundly right".[7]

For Coates, "The bible of Crosland revisionism, published in the mid-fifties, has dated more than any other important work of socialist analysis in the last fifty years. This means that Labour as a movement, as opposed to Labour as a potential government, can only exist on the basis of other doctrines, altogether more radical". This was a pressing and urgent need because for Coates, as much as for Benn and for Tories like Joseph and Thatcher, "It is manifest that the British status quo will be hard pressed to survive the decade, let alone longer".[8] He hoped that as that status quo broke down Britain would take the road of a reconstructed socialism based on industrial democracy. This did not seem totally unrealistic at the time. At Labour's 1973 Conference a composite resolution on Industrial Democracy was debated, with speakers from the floor and from the senior ranks of the party. The motion began by stating that "Conference welcomes the determination to extend public ownership and control, especially in the key growth sectors of the economy, but is convinced that for this policy to be carried through successfully, to win widespread support and to become the basis for fundamental changes in the social structure, strong and genuine elements of industrial democracy and workers' control will have to be introduced in all nationalised industries".[9]

The motion was a political litmus test. Roy Jenkins, disconcerted by conference delegates' enthusiasm for the concept, told them "We need to promise no more than we are convinced we can do", the obvious problem being that Roy Jenkins was not convinced he could do very much at all. Tony Benn, on the other hand, saw the application of industrial democracy within both state owned and private industry as an essential part of Labour's industrial policy and as a forerunner of a larger societal transformation. "We are offering much more than legislation" he said. "We are offering a perspective and a vision which will transform the political atmosphere of cynicism which has developed in recent years". The motion was passed by so big a margin that the vote wasn't even counted. In the event Labour did not even offer legislation, let alone a transfer of power within industry, but that failure was in the future.

For this reason and despite the suspicion with which trade union and Labour Party leaders regarded it, the forces of the political right were paranoid about the IWC. Coates was routinely labelled a Trotskyist and "Benn's guru" in the media and the IWC was subject to surveillance and infiltration by the Security Service (MI5, responsible for domestic counter-intelligence). Cathy Massiter, one of several MI5 "whistle-blowers", later revealed that the IWC's Treasurer Harry Newton was an MI5 asset who reported back on IWC activity.[10] Newton need not have bothered, as the IWC had no secret strategy or paymasters. Its proceedings, in line with its philosophy, were democratic and transparent. It reached the peak of its public profile and influence at a packed fringe meeting at the Labour Party's November 1974 Conference, attended and addressed by then Industry Secretary Tony Benn, who began his address to the gathering "The time has come for the Labour movement to intensify its discussion about industrial democracy". Benn expanded the argument from private to public corporations, saying that "In recent years many workers in nationalised industries have expressed their dissatisfaction with authoritarian management". He recommended a variety of experiments to address this, from worker's control to co-operatives to co-partnership. To counter concerns that in reality this would only produce a form of workers' capitalism, Mike Cooley, one of the convenors of the Lucas Aerospace Shop Stewards Combine, made clear that "We start from the simple premise that a direct conflict of interest exists between the employer and the workforce throughout Britain. We think that unless that is understood and unless workers build organisations powerful enough to meet force with force at the point of production, then they are simply creating illusions".[11]

After a wide ranging debate on the manner in which industrial democracy could be introduced throughout British society, and how this needed to be an integral part of the wider Social Contract which included the Labour Government's industrial strategy, Benn concluded "What stands out for me at any rate is the contrast between the confidence expressed at a meeting like this and the very widespread defeatism which is encouraged in our society".[12] Benn was referring to the British media's general trivia and cynicism rather than to specific political formations, although as Heath's government stumbled and fell there was a great deal of defeatism and pessimism on a British right frightened and demoralised by the string of trade union victories from 1971 to 1974. But whilst some of the Conservative Party and its traditional supporters were badly shaken they had resources to fall back on, most especially within the security services. The vast majority of MI5's senior officials had close social and professional connections to the Conservative Party, the City and the military. Not surprisingly they shared their political instincts and opinions.

These sympathies had come to the fore when the Heath government was confronted by overt and widespread opposition to the Industrial Relations Act in 1972. Initial approaches by Heath and Home Secretary Reginald Maudling to MI5 to bug meetings of the power workers' union at the Electricity Council were gently rebuffed by the liberal Cabinet Secretary Sir Burke Trend, who pointed out that the power workers were not subversive by any traditional definition.[13] But the successful defiance of the Industrial Relations Act changed the political landscape and led to the instalment of a new MI5 Director General, Michael Hanley, much more inclined to defer to the conspiracy theories of the right.

Chapter Four

Low Intensity Operations

One of the first things Hanley did upon appointment was to call a historic meeting of MI5's A and F Branches. A Branch dealt with Field Work and Technical Operations such as housebreaking, bugging and the "Watchers", MI5's surveillance agents based in Euston Tower. F Branch covered Domestic Counter Subversion including monitoring of trade unions, the CP, radical campaigning organisations and the media, and infiltrating agents into these. After gathering them together Hanley passed on a change in MI5's priorities. He told his staff that the Prime Minister and the Home Office wanted to increase the time and resources devoted to targeting "the far and wide left".[1] Unhappy with the passive role of the Joint Intelligence Committee – the usual interface between security services, other government departments and the Cabinet Office – Hanley suggested a new oversight committee under Home Office control to monitor subversion and "increasing industrial relations trouble". Hence the new Inter-Departmental Committee on Subversion in Public Life (SPL) was created in September 1972. SPL quickly got to work, co-ordinating reports from the Department of Employment with its own surveillance of those it regarded as "subversives". In the critical years 1972 and 1973 it produced reports for the Prime Minister on *Impact of Subversive Groups in Trade Union Activity*, *The Claimants and Unemployed Workers' Union*, *Labour Relations at Ford Motors*, *The Security Significance of the Ultra-Left in the UK in 1973*, and a series of separate reports on specific unions.[2]

The focus of MI5 and SPL on trade unions engaged in legal industrial action occurred at a time when disparate elements on the right were engaged in clearly dubious and illegal activities – activities which it would have been impossible for MI5 not to have known about as they were directed by current or former Security Service personnel. In February 1974, on the eve of a general election that was likely to return a Labour Party committed to an "irreversible shift in the balance of wealth and power in favour of working people", the right-wing journalist Chapman Pincher, often used as a catspaw by the Security Services, reported to his *Daily Express* readership that he was aware that a vigilante group "organised by former service chiefs, senior ex-members of the Secret Service and MI5" had been set up to "protect the country from a communist takeover".[3] Pincher was referring to Unison, a shadowy group set up by ex-Deputy Chief of MI5 George Kennedy Young, then a Conservative Party parliamentary candidate, and including senior ex-military figures such as Admiral Sir Ian Hogg and General Sir Walter Walker, NATO Commander-in-Chief of Allied Forces Northern Command 1969-1972. Upon retirement Walker had taken his military experience and network of contacts to Young and volunteered to put them to use in the struggle against internal subversion. Unison, and Walker's involvement with it, were revealed publicly in *The Times* in July 1974, which also revealed that the organisation was run by an inner committee of "bankers, businessmen and barristers".[4]

Unison seems to have seriously anticipated a possible military coup in response to Labour's election. This was not entirely wish fulfilment, given that MI5 had put Harold Wilson, Prime Minister of the UK for six years 1964-70, under official surveillance in the months preceding the February 1974 election. Some of these operations derived from Peter Wright's semilunatic suspicions of Wilson going back decades; some, though, was paranoid spin-off from Labour's political radicalisation during the early 1970s, a radicalisation that Wilson as Labour leader had to reflect in some way. At the last Labour Party conference prior to the February 1974 General Election Wilson had attacked the City for its lack of long-term support for British industry. Recommending Labour's plans for a National Investment Bank, Wilson called the City a "casino" that did not channel productive investment but devoted itself to "exaggerating the sloshing to and fro of the bilgewater of capitalism". He called for a reining in of speculative deals and a public inquiry into the workings of the Stock Exchange. Much of this was simply tacking left to appease the activists in his party, but elements within MI5 and its hangers on took him seriously and prepared for his re-election on that basis. It is unclear to this day how much of Unison's operations were actually planned and resourced and how much was feverish right-wing fantasy. Certainly Unison and its supporters – "bankers, businessmen and barristers" who had looked with approval on the military coup that removed Chile's socialist government in 1973 – were convinced that Tony Benn and the IWC were fronts for communism, and that any government that put Benn in a position of power might have to be dealt with in the same way.

These were not idle daydreams. In 1969 the British Army Land Manual added "domestic subversives" to its list of possible enemies, and with the re-emergence of the IRA in Northern Ireland, counter subversion was now a high priority. The influential 1971 book *Low Intensity Operations* by Brigadier Frank Kitson coolly explained the philosophy, strategy and tactics of urban counter insurgency and the military response to radical challenges to established power. Kitson outlined exactly how the British Army could undermine strikes and picket lines and how it would round up and detain those opposed to a joint military-civilian government in which "the law would be used as just another weapon".[5] He was soon sent off to Belfast to put his theories into practice which led to the Army's illegal collusion with "counter gangs" – loyalist thugs used to terrorise Catholic communities and crush the growing insurgency arising in Derry and Belfast. To assist the operation, the Army's Force Research Unit covertly provided Protestant paramilitaries with the names and addresses of Catholic activists.[6] Many of Kitson's other recommendations were taken forward by the newly established Information Policy Unit, "a disinformation and black propaganda operation"[7] which seemed to operate with no political control or accountability. Seemingly on its own initiative it created a covert operation called "Clockwork Orange" designed to smear and undermine those the Army considered a threat to the continued dominance of the Protestant majority in Northern Ireland – at first Catholic politicians from the Social Democratic and Labour Party (SDLP) and Sinn Fein, then Heath himself, and from 1974 mainly the British left and the Labour Party. The extent and effect of Clockwork Orange, in Northern Ireland and on British politics more generally, remains one of the great unmentionables of mainstream contemporary political history.

In a similar vein most on the political right supported the military coup that removed President Salvador Allende's democratically elected government and murdered up to 30,000 of its supporters. Speaking for them a few days after the coup *The Times* lead editorial of 15th September 1973 considered the rounding up of thousands of left-wing and trade union activists and their incarceration in the Santiago Football Stadium, where many were tortured and killed. It concluded that Allende's attempts to socialise the economy and redistribute national wealth had led to "ruin" and that "The circumstances were such that a reasonable military man could in good faith have thought it his constitutional duty to intervene". A few weeks later Ralph Miliband produced an analysis of the coup and the cold indifference of the Chilean and British ruling classes towards its victims, and drew appropriate conclusions for the left. Miliband urged that radical reforming governments must give "institutional content" to slogans about empowering workers. He advised any new regime bent on challenging capitalism to build and encourage "a network of organs of power, parallel to and complimenting the state power, and constituting a solid infrastructure for the timely mobilisation of the masses". He linked this explicitly to changes in personnel in the civil service, the military and the police.[8] Both Miliband and *The Times,* from entirely different perspectives, had gone to the heart of the issues created by General Pinochet's coup.

As Margaret Thatcher's life-long support for Pinochet demonstrated, *The Times* was simply articulating common right-wing political sentiment as well as Conservative government policy (the FCO gave explicit instructions to the British Embassy in Santiago that it not open its doors to those seeking sanctuary from the coup). Groups like Unison and GB75, set up by founder of the SAS Colonel David Stirling and intended to be a fast reaction strike breaking force, were led and covertly supported by people in significant positions within the military, the security services, and the City. They had formed in 1973-74 in direct response to the trade union challenge to Heath's government. They did not support Heath himself, on the contrary, they saw him as weak and centrist and yearned for a strong man (or woman) to lead the Tory Party from the right. Shortly before the February 1974 election Thatcher's political mentor, Airey Neave, led a group of Tory MPs including future Industry Secretary Norman Tebbitt to ask for Heath's approval to set up a "Civilian Volunteer Force" to assist the police with strike breaking, the "volunteer force" very likely to be drawn from the ranks of GB75.[9]

Tories like Neave reflected the worldview and increasing political paranoia of the leaders of British business. In 1972 the Deputy Director of the CBI had written to its member companies urging them to fund organisations that were investigating and combating what he called "subversion" within industry. Amongst these organisations were the Economic League, Aims of Industry and the Institute for the Study of Conflict (ISC). The ISC was set up and run by Brian Crozier, a fanatical anti-communist with a long and shadowy history on the fringes of the CIA, MI5 and the Conservative Party. Later in the 1970s he would establish an "advisory committee" called Shield that briefed Margaret Thatcher on security issues and offered advice on how to deal with the strikes and domestic unrest she would face in office if she instituted hard line monetarist policies. Based out of the offices of the Royal United Services Institute in Whitehall the ISC assumed a semi-academic veneer, but in reality it was "a British Intelligence operation under 'light cover'".[10] It received funding from Kern House Enterprises (a CIA front), the Ford Foundation and British firms such as Shell and BP, and delivered well attended lectures on the threat of left-wing subversion at Bramshill Police Training Academy, the Royal Military College of Science and the Army Staff College.

These were not simply fringe organisations floating extreme ideas. They were the outliers for a real shift of emphasis and policy within the British security services. Paul Foot's extensive investigations into Clockwork Orange and its poisonous effect on Irish and British politics concludes from an examination of reliable sources who broke ranks with MI5 and the Army's Information Policy Unit that at that time sections of MI5 were "motivated by reactionary ideas, and directed their considerable powers against the elected government they were meant to be serving".[11] Foot also cites MI5 whistleblower Cathy Massiter's belief that 1974 was "the year in which the mood in MI5 changed decisively" to an all out onslaught on what its senior officers perceived as revolutionary or subversive activity within the Labour Party, the trade unions and the wider left. Colin Wallace, the IPU officer whose notes and accounts of Clockwork Orange have never been seriously questioned, considers that "the intelligence community saw the situation in Northern Ireland as the front line of the left's threat to the UK, and of a great conspiracy by the communist bloc to undermine the whole of the UK".[12]

There is some evidence that planning for a military coup of the Chilean type – almost certainly with the same justification, already accepted by the *Spectator*, the *Times* and other pillars of the establishment – extended beyond a few right-wing MPs like Neave and paramilitary outfits like Unison and GB75. On 5th January 1974, as Britain's cities were plunged into nightly darkness by power blackouts, 400 troops of the Blues and Royals Guards regiment took over Heathrow Airport and set up checkpoints over a mile from the runways, sending separate patrols to Windsor and Eton. Although the ostensible reason for the exercise was to deter terrorists who may have acquired hand held rocket launchers, it was never explained why this would require the soldiers to take over the airport using Scorpion tanks and Saladin armoured cars, or what the other patrols were doing.[13] Heath felt it was an overreaction that would only exacerbate other tensions.

Heath himself did not seem to be privy to whatever the right wing of his own party was up to. But then his personal fate did not concern them. It was the manner of his government's passing that appalled right-wing conservatives such as Neave, Stirling and Young, for it would in the end be driven from office by highly successful industrial action. The trigger for Heath's demise was the beginning of the NUM's overtime ban in November 1973 in support of a pay claim, which once again broke the government's pay settlement ceiling. The government's rejection of the claim led to national strike action and a direct challenge to the Conservative government. As the country was hit by power blackouts Heath instituted a State of Emergency and in February 1974 called a General Election.

The story of the NUM's defeat of Heath and the "Who Governs Britain?" General Election has been told many times (the best and most nuanced account is in Andy Beckett's *When the Lights Went Out* (Faber & Faber, 2008), one of the few histories of the 1970s that examines the decade with freshness and objectivity).[14] The seeds were planted in May 1973 when over one and a half million workers had taken strike action to support a TUC

"Day of National Protest and Stoppage" against the government's pay restraint policy. From this emerged the entirely predictable response of the NUM and electricity workers to statutory pay restraint, namely a joint overtime ban beginning on 12 November 1973 and the government's panicked reaction a day later instituting a State of Emergency. A week later, the Secretary of State for Trade and Industry, Peter Walker, announced that petrol and fuel deliveries would be reduced by 10% in response to the overtime ban and sharply falling oil supplies from Arab oil states. On 13 December Heath announced that from the years' end all industries and commercial enterprises would be restricted to three consecutive days use of electricity each week. On 7th January 1974 the "Three Day Week" officially began.

After frantic but failed negotiations throughout January the NUM announced a strike beginning on 9th February. Threatened by the government with the imposition of a 2.5 days working week and the possible use of troops to work in the pits the Vice President of the NUM, Mick McGahey, broke decades of trade union evasion of overt class politics and declared "I will appeal for them to assist and aid the miners. Troops are not all anti-working class. Many of them are miners' sons – sons of the working class".[15] The reaction of the ruling class to this and to the strike was one of near hysteria. The media screamed that McGahey was trying to foment revolution. The Head of the Home Civil Service, William Armstrong, had a complete nervous breakdown and was found naked on his office floor ranting about communists.[16] He was swiftly removed from his position and sent to a rest home.

Ironically, many in the senior ranks of the Labour Party, including Harold Wilson, did not support the miners. Despite MI5 paranoia about him Wilson remained what he had always been – a morally flexible right-wing social democrat whose early dalliance with Nye Bevan had gifted him entirely undeserved "socialist" credentials. By 1974 those credentials were dust. He no longer spoke for or understood his own party members and activists, many of whom – after the politically galvanising events of 1970-74 – stood by the guiding statement of the February 1974 General Election Manifesto. *"The points set out in this Manifesto are Socialist aims, and we are proud of the word"* it began, before promising a fundamental and irreversible shift in the balance of wealth and power and of "making power in industry genuinely accountable to the workers and the community at large".[17]

Chapter Five

Social Contract

The result of the February 1974 election gave Labour 301 seats and the Tories 297. With Liberal and Nationalist MPs holding the balance Labour lacked a Parliamentary majority, making it difficult to pass politically controversial legislation.[1] Wilson was thus confirmed in his unspoken determination to quietly junk most of the radical economic proposals in the manifesto and to focus on the "Social Contract" that he had promised the nation he could deliver in tandem with Trade Union leaders, i.e. progressive social legislation to benefit working people in return for contained wage demands and industrial peace. The Social Contract had emerged from the work of the TUC-Labour Party Liaison Committee in a parallel process to the creation of the socialist industrial strategy. The prime mover was TGWU General Secretary Jack Jones who had initially sought an agreed programme between the unions and Labour to avoid the clashes and recriminations that had plagued the 1960s Labour governments. He therefore brought to the committee proposals for the repeal of the Industrial Relations Act, trade union recognition and consultation rights, and statutory rights for unions' health and safety representatives. Only as the programme grew in scope and significance did it become known as the Social Contract.

The trajectory of the Social Contract after 1976 (i.e. the unions contained their wage demands but received less and less for doing so) has obscured its initial appeal and success. Labour's October 1974 General Election Manifesto, re-emphasising the importance of the Social Contract as the party went again to the country to ask it for support, stated clearly that it was "not concerned solely or even primarily with wages. It covers the whole range of national policies. It is the agreed basis upon which the Labour Party and the trade unions define their common purpose".[2] The Social Contract in its entirety, laid out in the 1973 Programme, included a commitment to full employment, detailed regional planning to rejuvenate deprived areas, an extension of industrial democracy within industry including statutory requirements to disclose information to trade unions, and extended public ownership in shipbuilding, the ports, aircraft, North Sea Oil, land and financial institutions. It also included a range of progressive social policies in education, health and welfare including full comprehensive education, free nursery care and extended maternity benefits. In office some of these commitments would be honoured and some would not, and from 1976 the economic policy choices made by Labour's leadership made it impossible to deliver on the original vision; but for the TUC, Jones and Scanlon to support such a programme in partnership with a political party that appeared committed to deliver it was not a cynical strategy to contain industrial militancy. It was a mature and obvious choice.

Jones in particular had a wider vision for its application. Since the war, German trade unions had been partners in strategic decision-making within German industry and had secured the best welfare and employment rights in Europe outside of the "Nordic Model". In Britain this was unlikely to happen given the extremes of resistance to the idea of co-partnership from the CBI and some of the key unions. So Jones attempted to achieve the same outcomes through other means – a concordat with a Labour government that, in return for a measure of predictability on wages and industrial relations, would legislate into existence some of his pet ideas such as an official industrial relations conciliation service (to become ACAS) and a statutory body enforcing meaningful health and safety procedures at work (to become the Health and Safety Executive). He also helped to draft what would become the Employment Protection Act introduced in 1974 by Labour Secretary of State for Employment Michael Foot.[3]

The Social Contract revolved around the working partnership between Jones and Foot, who after decades of left-wing rebellion joined the Labour Opposition front bench in 1970. Jones "admired Foot for his sincerity and idealism, and as a rare example of a genuine socialist".[4] In return Foot respected a trade union leader who appeared very different from the right-wing block-vote wielding autocrats of the 1950s, who had used their power to stifle the Bevanites. Jones still retained a taste for the industrial syndicalism of his youth and was far more imaginative than most trade union leaders when it came to schemes for industrial and economic democracy within the workplace. When Foot became Shadow Leader of the House in 1971 the Jones-Foot axis was crucial in the creation of a union-party alliance. Jones later said, "I never doubted the value of the Social Contract, which I saw a major step towards economic equality and better conditions for working people, and used every democratic means to gain the co-operation of fellow trade unionists".[5]

Jones may have seen the Social Contract as a means to deliver "economic equality" but for Wilson it was simply a classic political trade off. Benn saw it mainly as a means of selling Holland's interventionist programme for industry and of providing an opening for industrial democracy. As such he underestimated the extent to which the industrial strategy could be, and was, subsumed within the Social Contract and thereby marginalised. This was the fatal flaw in the left's strategy for effecting "fundamental and irreversible change". Improvements to pensions and controls on prices were important but easily reversed. Fundamental reforms to the structure and ownership of British business were systemic changes of far more long term political and economic significance yet few in the government or the TUC, including Jones and Foot, recognised that without these essential elements the Social Contract would sooner or later become compromised and directionless.

Wilson and Benn were bound to clash but Wilson had little choice, given Benn's central role in formulating Labour's industrial policy since 1970, but to make him Secretary of State for Industry. With Michael Foot at the Department of Employment and Peter Shore at the Department for Trade, Benn led an ostensibly socialist bloc at the heart of a Labour Cabinet that still leaned to the right. The main offices of state – Chancellor, Foreign Secretary and Home Secretary – were held by Denis Healey, Jim Callaghan and Roy Jenkins, and it was these to whom Wilson usually deferred. This group of orthodox social democrats had virtually no political ideology to steer them except a progressive gradualism so slow it often went into reverse, allied to a terror of the markets and a loss of business "confidence" in a Labour government.

In 1974 they had much to be terrified about. The structural faultlines of the British economy, driven by the City's failure to support long-term investment in British firms and the dominance of financial and rentier values over wider social and industrial priorities, were paralysing growth and preventing innovation. Instead of research, reinvestment and restructuring most British companies would rather simply lay off workers, prompting industrial militancy in response.[6] Worse, the long term consequences of a little noticed decision by the Heath government in 1971 – the relaxation of Competition and Credit Control, which loosened the Bank of England's control of the ratio of bank's deposits to lending – were now being felt across the economy. Immediately after the changes the banks had massively expanded what were essentially fictional "reserve assets", resulting in an inflation and credit boom. Heath refused to raise interest rates to counter this and by the end of his government the rate of inflation was moving remorselessly up – it would rise from 10.2% in 1973 to 24.6% in 1975. This was a serious and continuous problem for the new Labour government. Despite being the root cause of the problem, the banks and the financial sector demanded more freedom to lend and speculate and resisted any attempt to re-impose the regulatory rules that had ensured stability since the war. Instead, they and their media allies placed the blame for economic crisis squarely at the feet of the trade unions' annual wage claims which were constructed merely to keep pace with the rise in the cost of living.

Westminster and the media rarely considered the lack of sustained reinvestment within British industry, or whether "patriotic" British banks prioritised such investment (they didn't). The Treasury's 1981 investigation of monetarist theory later concluded that inflation, the great bug bear of the 1970s, had little to do with wage demands and the money supply but mainly reflected the amount of credit the clearing banks were pumping in to the economy. To free themselves from their post-war dependence on the issuance and withdrawal of short term Treasury Bills British banks started to move in to the Euro Dollar market in the 1960s. Following deregulation of Credit Control in 1971 many started to lend and invest overseas, creating a serious balance of payments problem. There *was* a decline of British industry but it was traceable to a lack of investment and "the outflow of industrial and finance capital".[7] There were few effective remedies for this within a British economy dominated by the City. The most popular response on the right was to apply the slash and burn neo-liberal economics of Friedman and Thatcher, with destruction of older industries and mass unemployment used to contain wage demands. In 1974 Labour was not only opposed to this approach but committed to a fundamentally different one.

The British economy, and other European economies, was now struggling with the unprecedented problem of "Stagflation", the combination of stagnant growth *and* inflation, which conventional Keynesianism maintained were mutually exclusive. This was deemed by monetarist theorists to be a final repudiation of Keynes although in reality the explanation was quite clear. Since the Bretton Woods Agreement of 1944 (partially negotiated by Keynes for the British government) international exchange rates were based on a monetary system that tied each country's currency to the U.S dollar, which rested on its guaranteed convertibility to gold. This had given the global economy some stability and predictability and was the foundation for the post war "Golden Age" of welfare state capitalism. However, in the face of massive U.S public debt due to the costs of the Great Society programme and the Vietnam War, in 1971 President Nixon suspended dollar convertibility to gold. This ended Bretton Woods at a stroke and led to fluctuating exchange rates and a great increase in the power of currency traders and speculators to bet against specific currencies. On top of this the 1973 OPEC crisis in which the OPEC countries (not just the Arabs) had suddenly quadrupled the price of oil, led to price inflation unconnected to other factors such as growth or the lack of it.

In the panic of the OPEC crisis and rising inflation few stopped at the time to consider that the nature of the world economy and of national politics had changed fundamentally. In Keynes' view the most important outcome of Bretton Woods had been that it gave democratically elected governments the ability to restrict and control capital movements, and thus to plan and implement domestic economic policy according to other criteria (such as protection of employment and funding of social services) than simply the returns from trading floor deals. Without Bretton Woods there was created what has since been called a "Virtual Senate" of international traders and money manipulators who, with ICT to assist instant transfer of millions if not billions of dollars and sterling, can "conduct moment by moment referendums of government policies"[8] and if necessary pull the plug on those they dislike.

Social Democratic governments who wished to retain some

level of control over their economies and their ability to fund a generous welfare state were thus faced with severe new challenges. Without a means of reasserting control over the markets the focus shifted to domestic inflation. Given that inflation was a genuinely urgent problem there were only so many anti-inflationary policies a socialist government could endorse. Labour had already rejected a statutory incomes policy as unfair and divisive but it was committed to a voluntary one negotiated with the trade unions. In return for trade union pay "restraint" a Labour government would apply a countervailing series of social policies such as rent freezes, pension increases, and price controls. There were those in the Labour Party (and a vocal minority in the CP who criticised its prioritisation of industrial action) that regarded the Social Contract as a step forward from a strategy of pure industrial militancy based on econo-mistic wage demands, in that in return for contained annual pay claims from those in work it would deliver broader national policies of benefit to all working class people, i.e. women, who still tended to manage the domestic budget, care for children, and work fewer hours, the elderly and the unemployed. This was a controversial idea within a male dominated left and trade union movement, in which many members did not see why workers not responsible for the rampant inflation of 1973-74 should bear the burden of containing it.[9] Others, most especially Jack Jones, recognised that whatever its ultimate cause galloping inflation simply wiped out each years' annual pay increase and that unfettered collective bargaining on its own did not prevent that. Such was his authority that he brought the TUC and other unions with him.

It was in this economic context that the new government faced its first real moral and political test – how to respond to the new fascist regime in Chile, specifically whether to continue with an order placed with British shipyards by the Chilean navy for construction and delivery of two new battleships. These had been built and were awaiting dispatch to Chile where after the coup General Pinochet's military regime was imposing an extreme variant of neo-liberal monetarism, stripping Chilean workers of all rights, slashing wages to the bone and privatising most state assets for US multinationals to snap up cheaply. With many socialist and trade unionist activists murdered, imprisoned or under police surveillance, there was no opposition to Pincohet's experiment. Some of Milton Friedman's academic acolytes – the "Chicago boys", graduates of his economics course at Chicago University and now professional exponents of free market fundamentalism – had flown into Santiago to advise and support Pinochet. Under their tutelage the Chilean government cut social spending massively and unemployment rocketed. As a result of bankruptcies the state did not receive enough social security payments to maintain welfare services and only the charity of the Catholic Church's food banks kept starvation at bay. There was nothing complicated or nuanced about the Chilean military coup or its economic policy post-coup; "At its crudest, the Chicago programme was class vengeance".[10]

The fate of Chilean socialism was of great concern not only to the British labour movement but also to a progressive middle-class left that in the aftermath of Vietnam was increasingly alienated from the United States. *The Guardian* published three long articles in 1974 by Patrick Heron attacking American cultural imperialism, but it was military imperialism in Asia and Latin America that generated the most heat and anger. Soon after the coup the artists David Medalla and Cecilia Vicuna organised an "arts festival for democracy in Chile" at the RCA. British trade unions and the Labour Party provided funds, solidarity and succour to refugees from Pinochet. The Chilean TUC set itself up in exile in London and groups of shattered Chilean leftists congregated at the Centreprise bookshop and cafe in Hackney.[11] Many British trade unionists – with a class-consciousness sharpened by political upheavals at home and abroad – took proactive solidarity action. The most notorious was that taken by workers at the Rolls Royce factory in East Kilbride who blocked any work on eight Avon 207 jet engines intended for the Chilean Air Force's Hawker Hunter fighters. In March 1974 the factory's trade union representatives instructed their members to halt work on the engines and despite the protests of the Pinochet regime and legal threats brought by Rolls Royce against its workers, the engines sat and rusted for four years until one weekend they mysteriously disappeared.[12]

A small group of Scottish factory workers had demonstrated the obvious and most effective way for supporters of Chilean democracy to restrain Pinochet, i.e to boycott the country, to restrict trade and deny him military and economic supplies. The first thing the Labour government could have done was to refuse to deliver the new warships. Most Labour Party members wanted and expected the government to do this but Wilson and Foreign Secretary Jim Callaghan – responding to FCO advice and, as ever, agreeing with it – decided the order must be honoured and the ships sent. The outspoken socialist MP Eric Heffer was appalled. In 1972 he had taken a personal message of solidarity and support from Harold Wilson to President Allende and was impressed by Allende's commitment to achieving socialism through democratic, electoral means. Even though Heffer was a new government Minister (although not of Cabinet rank) he started to make public protests. Benn took the issue directly to Callaghan and cited Heffer's concerns. Callaghan's reply characterised his political type. He admitted that he "didn't understand it" and told Benn that Heffer "had better be careful" if he wished to continue as a Minister. At Cabinet he stressed the "major export interest" that was involved.[13] When it came to a vote even other left Ministers like Barbara Castle and Peter Shore stayed silent, with only Benn and Foot voting against fulfilling the order. To the anger and dismay of Labour party members the warships were sent.

Chapter Six

Power Sharing

Benn had to accept defeat on Chile. But within his own domain of industrial policy he made it clear that he would be fully implementing the policies on which the Labour Party had stood for election. He was determined to set up the National Enterprise Board to channel funds to industry, and to institute Planning Agreements to give the Labour government greater control over strategic investment and open the door to the kind of industrial democracy advocated by the IWC. His first meetings with his departmental officials, led by the Permanent Secretary Sir Anthony Part, did not go well. Part's opening words to the new Secretary of State for Industry were "I presume, Secretary of State, that you do not intend to implement the industrial strategy in Labour's programme?". Benn told him that he did indeed intend to implement it. In his diary Benn admitted to himself that he would face huge opposition within Whitehall and he needed to counteract that by cultivating external allies: "One of my biggest jobs is to make contact with the shop stewards movement, and if I do that I am going to run into difficulties not only with the Cabinet, the Right and the press, but also with trade union leaders".[1]

Benn was not entirely alone. He had firm party allies working for him in the department – the socialist MPs Eric Heffer and Michael Meacher were appointed his Minister of State and Parliamentary Under Secretary and he had also brought reliable political advisors with him. The combative former trade union activist Heffer, in particular, was seen by the political Right and the media generally as even more dangerous than Benn. The *Times* reported that senior civil servants in the Industry Department were "horrified" when at a meeting to draw up industrial strategy Heffer had bluntly told them the manifesto must be translated in to government policy.[2] Benn may have had Heffer as stalwart support and to a lesser extent a few Cabinet allies such as Foot at Employment (though Foot's main focus was to deliver the Social Contract and keep Jones and Scanlon on board, in pursuit of which he would and did compromise on many other things) but he was encircled by political enemies from his first day in office. One of the most perceptive analyses of Benn and the Labour "New Left" found that "...an alliance quickly emerged between senior civil servants in Benn's department and centre-right Labour Ministers and their Permanent Secretaries, with the Treasury at the hub, to have the industrial strategy aborted by Cabinet before it saw the light of day". Denis Healey's special assistant Adam Ham later revealed there was a "Whitehall-wide conspiracy to stop Benn doing anything".[3]

That "Whitehall" would organise to stop Benn says much about its priorities at a time when the new government was assailed on all sides. The first overt challenge to its legitimacy arose in Northern Ireland. The introduction by the Northern Ireland government in 1971 of Internment without trial had been a massive own goal leading to rioting and the establishment of "Free Derry", an area of Londonderry sealed by IRA barricades and a no-go area for the Army and RUC. In January 1972 British paratroopers opened fire on an unarmed Catholic civil rights march and killed 13 people, five shot in the back, in what was to become known as Bloody Sunday. The UK government then suspended the Stormont government and reasserted Direct Rule from London. The IRA responded on 21st July 1972 by setting off twenty-six bombs in 80 minutes in central Belfast. Faced with possible civil war in the province even the Conservatives perceived the need to offer the Catholic minority a reason to believe in the political process or recruitment to the IRA would continue to rise. The result was the Sunningdale Agreement between the British Government, the Irish Government and the Northern Irish Executive (all that was left under Direct Rule) as well as representatives of Northern Irish Catholics such as the Social Democratic and Labour Party (SDLP). Sunningdale established a "power sharing" Executive that whilst still run by the moderate Protestants of the Ulster Unionist Party under Brian Faulkner for the first time guaranteed places for Catholic representatives. It also involved a degree of cross border co-operation with Dublin through the newly created Council of Ireland set up as a result of pressure from the SDLP and its socialist leader Gerry Fitt.

These reforms, supported and carried further by the newly elected Labour government, ran up against a wall of resistance from extremist Protestant politicians such as Ian Paisley and paramilitaries like the Ulster Defence Force (UDF). This led to the Ulster Workers Council strike of May 1974 in which many Protestant workers across the province (though not in the Harland and Wolf Shipyard, where more politically conscious workers voted against a strike that had nothing to do with trade unionism or labour solidarity) downed tools with the single demand – scrap the power sharing Executive and return to the gerrymandered Northern Irish electoral system that had started the Troubles in the first place. The British Army, ever supportive of the Ulster Protestants, resisted efforts by London to get them to break the strike and exhibited open co-operation with the UDF on blockades and picket lines. There seems little doubt now that the strike was "used by MI5 and the Army as part of the destabilisation campaign"[4] against the new Labour Government which they perceived as committed to total withdrawal from Northern Ireland. It was true that the Northern Ireland Secretary Merlyn Rees was conducting secret negotiations with the IRA but then so had his Conservative predecessor. Nothing less than defeat of power sharing and a humiliating retreat by the government would satisfy the Protestant ultras, and this they achieved.

Wilson and Rees quickly dropped power sharing and the chances of a "peace process" that would bring Protestant and Catholic politicians together around the same table was put back two decades.

The UWC strike had diverted the new government's time and energies just when it needed to get to grip with urgent political and economic issues. It had also demonstrated, by the reluctance of MoD civil servants to authorise the movement of more troops to Ulster to break the strike, how far the "permanent government" might go to frustrate the elected one.[5] On other fronts Whitehall was less obstructive and in its initial days the Wilson government delivered some impressive radical reforms. The new government rapidly raised old age pensions and rent subsidies and began to build new council houses to address the housing shortage. It repealed the hated Housing Finance Act that had ratcheted up rents and created a homeless underclass, and followed that with an imposed rent freeze. On public ownership the government moved quickly to nationalise the aircraft and shipbuilding industries. Unfortunately, although the initial moves to nationalise shipbuilding into British Shipbuilders (BS) were taken in 1974 the protracted determination of appropriate compensation for shareholders meant that the final transfer from private to public did not take place until 1977, by which time Tony Benn was no longer Industry Secretary. This meant that BS became a standard public corporation run solely for the bottom line with no involvement from its workforce or attempts made to diversify production other than plant closures. Thus set up, BS was a sitting duck for the privatisers of the Thatcher government who in any case had a visceral hatred for the working class culture of the Scottish and northern shipyards.[6]

In his first three days in office, 5-7 March, Michael Foot at the Department of Employment settled the outstanding issues of the Miners' strike. He called in the NUM leaders, told them that the previous government's pay limit no longer applied and free collective bargaining was restored, and then passed the NUM pay claim back to the Coal Board with instructions to negotiate an immediate settlement. The board took the hint and agreed the claim. Coal deliveries resumed and the Three Day Week was ended. After resolving the immediate cause of the industrial discontent Foot moved quickly to sweep away the previous statutory incomes policy and repeal the Industrial Relations Act. He also oversaw the introduction of the Employment Protection Act and the Sex Discrimination Act which would provide ordinary workers with valuable protections against the "hire and fire" culture of the worst companies and the most arrogant managers.[7]

Much of Foot's legislative record in 1974-76 before he was moved to become Leader of the House and Deputy Prime Minister was impressive and of lasting impact, but the same cannot be said of his response to escalating unemployment. In 1972 unemployment had topped one million for the first time since the 1930s. With British industry contracting unemployment was still rising and a Labour government committed to the Social Contract was duty bound to address it if it could. An effective response would have benefited from a joined up approach between the Departments of Employment and Industry but Foot and Benn, buried in immense and immediate pressures and struggling to pass significant new legislation, do not seem to have formulated one. Benn's excuse would have been that he was increasingly constrained by Wilson in what he could do within his own department, let alone another one. Foot's would be that once he settled the problems left over from the previous government he did move to introduce new unemployment schemes such as a recruitment subsidy to encourage public sector employers to take on school leavers, a £30million job creation scheme for the Manpower Services Commission, and job creation arising from enhanced government building projects. The programme was not enough. It was piecemeal, it did not focus strategically on fostering new industries and emerging technologies, and it lacked real funds. Labour's complacency on unemployment would return to haunt it.

Easily the most controversial part of the DoE programme was the new trade union legislation enshrined in the Trade Union and Labour Relations (TULRA) Act and the Employment Protection Act. Foot's aim was to "recast the framework of industrial law"[8] but in that he was only partially successful. The Acts were a useful corrective to the massive imbalance of power within industry between employer and employee, and delivered what were uncontroversial and standard trade union freedoms in many other European countries. But they were essentially a reaction to external threats, not a new institutional structure to permanently embed trade unions into the decision making process and make it difficult to dislodge their influence. In the 1980s Thatcher would demonstrate how comparatively easy it was to reverse these rights and tie up the unions in legal constraints that were "the most restrictive on trade unions in the western world".[9]

Other European Socialist parties such as the Swedish Social Democratic Party (SAP) had more ambitious plans. In the early 1970s the SAP and the Swedish Trade Union Confederation had undergone a process of radicalisation similar to that of the British Labour Party, driven by "rank and file militancy of the late 1960s, the student movement, the New Left, and the wildcat strikes of 1969...".[10] This led to new thinking about how to extend the power of labour over capital and specifically to the proposals of the Swedish Wage Earners Fund or Meidner Plan (after its creator Rudolf Meidner, the architect of the Swedish post-war Welfare State). It was long-term investment in public infrastructure and social services that had guaranteed the prosperity and high quality of life of the Scandinavian Welfare States. Private management had been left intact. The Meidner Plan was a scheme whereby private firms with more than 50 employees would have to issue new shares every year equivalent to 20% of its "excess profits", these to be channelled to "Wage Earner Funds" managed by employees and local authorities. The Funds could not sell the shares but they could re-invest the yield for future social spending. In a country with 80% trade union membership this meant their unions would accrue an escalating amount of shares in the Fund until they attained majority control of the firm. It was a stronger variant on the Social Contract in that in return for control over the investment decisions of the firm the unions might occasionally contain wage demands, if only to safeguard employment and profit share at a later date. The Funds would gradually replace private with employee and semi-public ownership but safeguard the cash flow and resources the firm needed to reinvest and survive.

Despite the Plans' intention to protect profit accumulation it was the *distribution* of wealth and profit that worried Swedish business, who looked on the Meidner Plan with such horror that "they were no longer sure if capitalism had a future in social-democratic Sweden".[11] As it transpired it did, as the SAP lost power in 1976 before it could legislate for the Wage Earners Fund. By the time it recovered power in 1981 the political atmosphere had altered enough that Swedish employers could successfully threaten boycotts and capital flight if the Plan was fully implemented. A weaker version requiring a levy from employees (i.e a pay cut to start it off) was pushed through in 1983 by an alliance of the SAP and Swedish Communist Party but it was in the form of pilot schemes that were never renewed. The Meidner plan has been called *"the most far sighted attempt to think through the types of new finance that would be needed to guarantee generous social provision"* in a developed welfare state,[12] and to establish firm rules whereby private corporations channelled their profits into public services and were slowly socialised as they did so.

Very few people in the British labour movement of the 1970s, beyond the IWC and some of the "Euro Communist" reformers within the Communist Party, were seriously thinking through the practical requirements of a legislative challenge to corporate control of investment and its subsequent distribution of wealth. For most of the left a challenge to corporate capitalism was expressed either as a total transformation of society, the specifics of which remained hazy, or as an understandable but inchoate desire to simply Tax the Rich (sadly, the same could be said today). For all the energy and impact of its first legislative programme the intellectual atmosphere inside the new Labour government was still that of 1964 or even 1945. The only senior Labour figure who was thinking outside these boxes was Tony Benn at the Department for Industry.

Chapter Seven

A Cold Coup

In its first months in office the Labour government had introduced substantial and useful reforms that improved the quality
of life of many people. In significant ways they edged British
society leftward and as such were resisted and condemned by the
right and much of the media. But in the main they conformed to
an accepted model of paternalistic social democracy and were not
too much of a departure for the civil servants that had to
implement them. At the Department of Industry things were
quite different. Upon arrival at the Department Benn had
immediately replaced a painting of British imperial triumph
hanging behind the Secretary of State's desk with a huge and
colourful trade union banner. He made it clear to his officials that
that he saw his primary constituency as the workers and trade
unions that had supported him and elected Labour to power. In
March he informed Sir Kenneth Keith, Chairman of Rolls Royce,
that he intended to meet Rolls Royce shop stewards before he met
him.[1] In April, when the Meriden Triumph Motorcycle company
(part of the NVT motorcycle conglomerate) was looking at
bankruptcy and its local unions asked for support to run the firm
themselves, Benn met Meriden workers in his office. He assisted
in the creation of a workers co-operative part funded by his
department and made it plain that the shop stewards could see
him whenever they liked.

Throughout his time at Industry he sought to channel money
to Meriden and other workers co-operatives such as Kirkby
Manufacturing and the *Scottish Daily News*, seeing these initiatives as not only generating employment but laying the ground
work for "a new form of decentralised, worker controlled social
ownership"[2] that did not replicate the 1945 model of nationali-

sation. Benn ensured that Meriden was incorporated as a separate entity so that it could avail itself of £4.96 million of subsidy from the DoI and not be tied to NVT. For Benn the setting up of a workers' co-operative at Meriden was an important step in developing his libertarian socialism for it "resolved the paradox between extending 'socialisation' of the economy with the commitment to extending industrial democracy".[3] The occupation at Fisher Bendix in Merseyside had also led workers to demand more from their environment and employment and they approached the DoI for help in setting up a co-operative. All Benn's proposals to support new ownership initiatives and to channel small amounts of government funds to workers' co-ops (he had personally dispatched a DoI Accountant to assist the Meriden workers draw up their financial plans) were fiercely resisted by his departmental officials, although far higher sums had recently been handed over to the City to buffer it against financial mismanagement – and would be again.

The internal wrangling over funding workers co-operatives were skirmishes, a prelude to the bigger battle to pass a substantive Industry Act that would create a powerful National Enterprise Board with a remit to institute real, effective Planning Agreements across industry. Though it was clearly Labour Party policy and a key part of the 1974 Manifesto Benn found very little support from his own colleagues and unremitting resistance within Whitehall. In retrospect, given the deep scepticism of the new Prime Minister and Chancellor he had little chance to get through a White Paper that would prepare the ground for a wide-ranging and meaningful Industry Act. But Benn did not see it that way. He felt himself beholden to the party and the policies on which it had been elected and regardless of vehement opposition he had a duty to implement those policies. He and Heffer brought copies of the 1973 Programme and the Manifesto into the Industry Department and circulated them to officials, as the blueprint of what they wanted from the White Paper. Benn then set up a Working Group led by Heffer whose task it was to provide him with a full draft, which he would bring to the Cabinet.

The Working Group was the centre of the storm. As well as Heffer it included Benn's personal advisor, the left-wing economist Frances Morrell. It also included Stuart Holland who had a government position as Economic Advisor to the Minister for Overseas Development Judith Hart, a radical socialist herself and a long time obsession of MI5 who considered her a covert communist. Benn had asked Holland to sit on the Working Group to steer through what were in many respects his ideas. Filled out with senior Industry Department experts, the Working Group set itself a tight timetable to give Benn a workable draft. On 1st April Heffer put his own draft of the White Paper to the Group to consider and from there progress was rapid despite the blank refusal of DoI officials to draft the parts relating to the NEB as these were deemed "political".[4] As the draft filled out it became clear that the Working Group had powerful enemies who did not want to see it produce anything of substance. Sir Anthony Part "believed the proposals were so politically interventionist that they would alienate every section of industry and that without that support the government's industrial strategy was doomed",[5] blind or more likely indifferent to the fact that being interventionist *was* the government's industrial strategy. Denis Healey was also concerned to reassure business leaders that it was their priorities, rather than Labour policy, that were his primary concern. Within his own domain he told Treasury officials that he believed plans for nationalisation were inflationary and he would oppose them.

Although Benn had kept Healey's officials off the Working Group its deliberations were passed to the Treasury by sympathetic Industry Department officials and Benn's ministers suspected that "The Treasury was waging a skilful campaign against the proposals to be incorporated in the draft White

Paper".[6] The internal battle became more frenzied in May when Benn responded to a request from the liaison committee that linked the Parliamentary Party, the NEC and the TUC for an update from all Cabinet Ministers on progress thus far. Benn's detailed reply, which promptly leaked to an overwhelmingly hostile media, restated that the proposals for the White Paper flowed from Labour's Programme 1973 and pledged that the NEB would rationalise the structure of the main industrial sectors "in line with the longer-term public need, rather than short term considerations", i.e. of immediate shareholder return. Worse, from the perspective of Wilson, Healey, Part and the CBI, he added that the government would face down the economic power of multinational companies "by empowering a tougher bargaining stance for government, particularly over new investment location".[7]

Benn's report made it clear that the guiding principle of Labour's industrial strategy was to use the NEB and the Planning Agreements to ensure "the conformity of the leading companies with national economic priorities" and that to do this the government would intervene as required – on price control, regional employment policy and investment, product development and industrial relations. One part of this process was to fundamentally transform relations between central government and the trade union movement so that "the same close relations that now exist between this department and management will exist with the unions, as it already does with the Department of Employment". Nor was this simply an aspiration. The report explicitly committed the Ministers of the DoI to "a major campaign of public explanation and discussion" to sell the policy, to be led by Heffer, Cripps and Holland.[8] Nothing like this had been attempted before. Benn's report laid the groundwork not just for legislation but also for a grass roots campaign to support that legislation. It promised that "we shall undertake a series of meetings in major cities throughout the country at which we would hope to meet trade union officials, representatives of local employers associations, local authorities, shop stewards" and others who could help the policy succeed. Given Benn's already demonstrated preference for industrial democracy, the CBI reacted with horror.

In steering the proposals through Whitehall the ex trade union negotiator Heffer, although not compromising on the core of the proposals, had favoured less confrontational language. Benn, however, was afraid that ambiguity would weaken them and so he inserted bolder terms and an overt political perspective. This was a tactical mistake. Wilson was already suspicious and nervous of what the Working Group was going to produce. He now ordered that when complete the draft White Paper be sent to him before it proceeded any further. Heffer and Benn had done the best they could with it and despite resistance from DoI officials it now reflected the policies of the election manifesto. But once it left Industry and passed to the Cabinet Office the White Paper was in the hands of those who felt no obligation to deliver Labour Party policy as decided by the NEC and Conference. From the moment Wilson and the Cabinet Office took control of the final draft the possibility that they would produce an Industry Act truly reflective of Stuart Holland's vision was almost zero. Wilson, the New College, Oxford Economic History Don, was horrified at what he read, criticising it later as "redolent more of an NEC Home Policy Committee document than a Command Paper".[9] He ordered a thorough re-write by Cabinet Office officials.

It is unclear exactly who revised the draft. It appears to have been a joint effort between Wilson's officials and Michael Foot, who was under instructions from Wilson and Healey to keep the final White Paper within strict parameters they had laid down. Foot seems to have kept his role to himself (he never informed Benn) possibly because he knew that he was watering down not only Benn's work but the agreed policies of the national party, and possibly because he did not really grasp the importance of the industrial strategy. When the revised paper was discussed in Cabinet on 2nd August Benn had to fight a rearguard action to preserve the essentials of the policy. Whilst he did retain elements that Healey and Callaghan wished removed he did not succeed in convincing the Cabinet to legislate on the basis of the full industrial strategy as laid out in the 1973 Programme and the 1974 Manifesto, although inexplicably he did not seem to fully realise that at first.[10]

The White Paper, published on 15th August as *The Regeneration of British Industry*, was a lesser version of the draft that had left the Industry Department Working Group. The essential directing role of the Planning Agreements was virtually removed as they had lost the element of command and control. The Agreements that were central to the strategy would now be merely voluntary. The NEB itself had less power than originally intended and less finance to back it up. The Working Group's draft had given the NEB the power to take over firms that were deemed to be failing in their responsibilities to their workforce and to wider society, as well as to take over bankrupt firms and to create new state enterprises.[11] In the White Paper the NEB could still nationalise but its remit to do so was constrained. It would, in any case, operate within normal stock exchange procedures (the "sloshing to and fro of the bilgewater of capitalism" as Wilson had put it a few months before) rather than challenge and reform those procedures. As the White Paper went through a gruelling procedure in the Committee stages of the House of Commons and the House of Lords Benn, Heffer and Holland realised that they were likely to secure a pale shadow of what they aimed for, yet they could not make that clear to either supporters or enemies without publicly criticising the Labour Prime Minister. It was, as Ken Coates put it later when analysing the government's failure to advance its own industrial policy, "a cold coup".

Throughout late 1974 and early 1975 Benn and Heffer painstakingly steered the Industry Act through its Parliamentary stages, secretly suggesting to left-wing backbench Labour MPs that they add amendments to drag it back to something more like Holland's original conception. But no matter how they manoeuvred they were trapped by political circumstances. By their continued presence at Industry they gave hope to trade union and party activists that genuinely significant reforms were being implemented. On the other hand such was their demonic reputation in the Tory press that they "ensured British capital's continued and vociferous hostility to even the watered down legislation".[12] Despite this serious setback for the left the CBI and the right-wing media were still frenzied in their opposition. Benn was savaged almost daily as a power mad Marxist who threatened parliamentary democracy by a press that did not investigate or condemn the anti-democratic views and activities of the new Conservative Party leadership. In July the right-wing political columnist Walter Terry had suggested in the *Daily Express* that Benn and Foot aided by trade union allies were aiming for a government similar to Salvador Allende's – in Terry's terms, a Marxist government that threatened democracy. This fundamentally misrepresented both Allende's government and the internal politics of the Labour government, in which Foot allied with Scanlon and Jones strove to introduce progressive reforms to social benefits and employment rights in return for trade union pay restraint, whilst Benn and his allies looked for more radical solutions, often to union leaders' dismay.

Tories such as Thatcher, Neave and Nicholas Ridley were now openly supportive of fascist rulers like Pinochet. Even a moderate Conservative such as Ian Gilmour (later sacked by Prime Minister Thatcher for not being "one of us") wrote in an elegant restatement of conservative philosophy that "Conservatives do not worship democracy. For them, majority rule is a device... and if it is leading to an end that is undesirable or inconsistent with itself then there is a theoretical case for ending it".[13] Gilmour himself would probably have been aghast at a British Pinochet but many others on the right would not. The half-buried current of far-right activity that emerged in 1973-74 in reaction to the upsurge of trade union militancy had not evaporated. If anything it had intensified since Labour took office on an avowedly socialist manifesto. Wilson's personal secretary, Marcia Williams, later confirmed that in August 1974 she and Wilson believed there was a real risk of a military coup of some kind and that they both would be arrested along with the rest of the Labour Cabinet.[14] They had been badly shaken in June when the Army staged another occupation of Heathrow Airport without informing Wilson that it was about to do so. The exercise was followed by an article in the *Times* by Lord Chalfont (who in the House of Lords expressed alarm about the work of the IWC and its links to Tony Benn) exploring how a hypothetical military coup might come about if the circumstances demanded it.[15] Revolution and Counter Revolution may or may not have been on the cards, but they were certainly in the air.

Chapter Eight

Children of the Revolution

Britain's ruling class was nervous, and not simply because radical socialists had mysteriously ended up running the Department of Industry. After the destruction of the Sunningdale Agreement the IRA had taken the war to the mainland which led to bombs in London, Guildford and Birmingham (although the appalling pub bombings in Birmingham in November 1974, which killed twenty one people and resulted in an upsurge of anti-Irish feeling in Britain, seem to have been a rogue operation unsanctioned by its leadership). The international outlook was also worrying. In 1974 socialist and social democrat governments were in office across Europe, in Germany, Denmark, Belgium, Austria, the Netherlands, Sweden and Finland. At the same time Franco's dying regime in Spain was rocked by mass strikes. In Greece massive popular opposition would soon overthrow the military Junta that had ruled the country since 1967. In April 1974 the Portuguese fascist leader Salazar's successor Caetano was overthrown by the Armed Forces Movement (MFA) led by politically liberal junior officers on a programme of "Democracy, Development and De-Colonisation". For the next year as the "Carnation Revolution" ebbed and flowed it seemed possible that a Marxist government might establish itself in Lisbon.

With Caetano gone many socialist and communist political exiles returned home. In May 1974 workers in the state owned airline TAP demanded the removal of all managers who had been appointed by the previous fascist regime and election of union representatives to the TAP governing council. Even though the provisional government that had taken over after Caetano's fall and held power in uneasy alliance with the MFA was composed of Socialist and Communist Party ministers as well as centrist liberals, it did not like to see rank and file workers taking the initiative on their own. It sent the army in to take over the airport and arrest the strikers but this did not stop a wave of factory and farm occupations convulsing Portugal. The Movement of Left Socialists (MES), a group of socialist and catholic activists who dissociated themselves from the provisional government, began to campaign amongst the union rank and file for a thorough going transformation of Portuguese society.[1] As a result of the agitation of the MES and the Proletarian Revolutionary Party (PRP) workers in many enterprises moved outside the bureaucratic union structures and elected their own committees to represent them. By October 1974 thousands of such committees had sprung up and by summer 1975 hundreds of factories were being run as self-managed co-ops, a spontaneous form of workers control that in the UK found expression in the work of the IWC and the attempts by Tony Benn to link workers' co-ops to Labour's industrial strategy. At the same time many of Portugal's poor and unemployed had began to take over empty property in Lisbon and elsewhere, co-ordinated by Autonomous Revolutionary Neighbourhood Committees of local residents who organised the use of empty property not only as homes but as community centres, crèches and communal services. In one sense it was a politicised form of the squatters movement in the UK and mass occupations like Tolmers Square.

Although by the end of 1975 the fragmented Portuguese left had lost the initiative and constitutional capitalism reasserted itself, the fall of Portugal's colonial rulers had a destabilising effect in Africa. Revolutionary situations were created in its former colonies Angola and Mozambique, where new national liberation movements waged guerrilla campaigns against those who had profited from colonialism and their South African allies. In the ex-British colony of Jamaica an experiment in peaceful democratic socialism had obvious parallels with developments in the UK, both in the style and content of the political challenge posed to domestic elites and the manner in which the institutions of global capitalism responded to it.

Elected to office in 1972 on a large parliamentary majority Michael Manley's radical People's National Party (PNP) promised a new beginning for Jamaica. Its programme included nationalisation of the foreign owned electricity, telephone and bus companies, relaxation of press and literary censorship, the provision of free secondary education, compulsory recognition of trade unions and long overdue pay increases for nurses, teachers and civil servants.[2] Manley himself was a determined and moralistic socialist not unlike Tony Benn. In a speech in 1974 he identified his political philosophy as a direct repudiation of the capitalist development model, stating that "If we accept economic growth is not an objective in itself but a result to be desired to the extent that it creates the conditions within which to pursue full employment and a rising standard of living for everyone, then we have introduced an important new criterion against which to measure our planning options".[3] Manley overstepped the line in his challenge to the region's Superpower when in January 1974 he announced he would remove tax breaks and other financial deals enjoyed by US and Canadian Bauxite companies in Jamaica. The CIA, already deeply suspicious of the PNP, began to foment political dissent and to fund opposition parties. Manley was in danger of following Allende to an early grave.

In the middle of the 1970s the UK saw its own version of how a socialist presence at the heart of government could stimulate new attitudes about wealth, power and culture. In April and May 1974 the League of Socialist Artists and the Artists Union worked together to mount an exhibition of paintings about the miners called "United We Stand" at Congress House, TUC Headquarters in London. Conrad Atkinson's ICA exhibition "Work, Wages and Prices" used photomontage to display and juxtapose photos of people at work, their wage slips, and print outs of stock exchange prices and profits. Paul Wombell's 1975 "Air India" simply placed two photos side by side – an advertisement for Air India of a glamorous stewardess in a sari offering "a glimpse of India" with a photo of a tired female Asian cleaner at Heathrow captioned "a glimpse of exploitation". This was fairly blunt agit-prop but it reflected a growing trend amongst artists of using photo-journalistic techniques to make a political point, a technique used with some skill in a controversial work by the left-wing conceptual artist Victor Burgin. Burgin, drawing equally from Marx, Foucault, Barthes and Andy Warhol, brought a subversive sensibility to the deconstruction of texts and advertising. His powerful *Les Feng* at the Lisson Gallery May-June 1974, comprised nine prints of the same glossy advertisement for Harvey's Bristol Cream in which an affluent couple sip sherry to toast their model daughter's appearance on the cover of *Vogue,* with parallel text against each image about a Vietnamese village leaders' lifetime of work for his community.[4]

Radical humanistic alternatives to dominant systems of thought were springing forth in all areas. In 1975 the American theoretical physicist Fritjof Capra, living and working in London since 1971, wrote *The Tao of Physics,* a ground breaking attempt to synthesise the tenets of Eastern mysticism with relativistic sub-atomic particle theory. To do so Capra started from the discovery that atomic particles were not separate entities but probability patterns whose position or wave function was entirely dependent on the intervention of the observer. In that sense, therefore, "reality" was based not on fixed points but dynamic interconnected processes not unlike the holistic "web of life" of Hinduism and Taoism. The book became a cult hit purely by word of mouth and went on to be an international bestseller. Capra would develop these ideas further in *The Turning Point* (1981) which criticised both corporate capitalism and Stalinist socialism as inflexible mechanistic philosophies based on hierarchy, patriarchy, aggression and constant expansion. He claimed that a more holistic, co-operative, and ecological "systems theory" approach to social and economic policy was emerging from the countercultures of the 1960s and 1970s. At the same time as Capra published his first book, the British scientist James Lovelock was developing his highly influential "Gaia hypothesis" which posited the Earth as a complex inter-active system that functioned as one organism, and urgently required a less exploitative approach to its natural resources if its eco-system – in which humanity resides – was to survive. Although some of these insights would melt into the pleasant vacuities of New Age sub-cults, Lovelock and Capra, working in Britain in the middle of the 1970s, had laid the philosophical foundation of the emerging Green movement.

Such "paradigm shifts" were not confined to the higher reaches of art and science. In the 1960s The Beatles had metamor-phosed from mop tops to hippies in very short time before elevating themselves into non-existence. In their wake a wave of musical rebels and aesthetes emerged under the broad heading of Glam Rock, which could be outrageously camp and crude but also included and redefined elements of avant-garde art, English dandyism and sexual transgression. Whilst Glam came to be defined in the popular imagination with barnstorming enter-tainers like Sweet and Slade, its real powerhouse and enduring influence was in stylistic innovators like Marc Bolan and T Rex, Roxy Music, and David Bowie. Although Bowie and Roxy Music would produce outstanding work in the 1980s (Bolan was killed in a car crash in 1977) it was during the early to mid 1970s that they established their artistic credentials, and in "Children of the Revolution" T Rex arguably produced the anthem of the subversive counterculture of 1970s Britain.

Although Glam would implode in self-parody, platform soles and the epic mediocrity of the Bay City Rollers, its colour and energy defined the early and middle years of the decade. With the soaring *Out of the Blue* (1977) ELO demonstrated that the genre could transcend its conventions and still dominate the British music scene in popularity and sales at a time when Punk supposedly defined the anger and despair of the period. Punk undeniably caught and expressed the frustrations and discontent of many young people in the late 1970s but at first "It seemed to be flailing, its anger inarticulate, its targets indiscriminate".[5] Even at its apogee Punk was contested by Disco – *Saturday Night Fever* was certainly more popular with working class youth than *Never Mind the Bollocks*.[6] Punk's best bands such as The Clash and The Jam quickly outgrew its furious nihilism and found their own style, while The Sex Pistols flamed and died. With the art school propaganda of Punk now receding into history, it is clear that for the bulk of the 1970s it was the fundamentally positive message of Glam and Disco that appealed to the British pop music audience – from Bolan's sleek and assertive "Get it On" and "20th Century Boy", to the energy and hyper-intelligence of Bowie's "Jean Genie" and "Rebel, Rebel", to the blue collar feminism of Suzi Quatro's "Can the Can" and the experimental techno rush of Donna Summers' "I Feel Love".

In their different ways all of these artists broke boundaries but it was Bowie, in his adopted personas and his sexual ambiguity, who most exemplified and flaunted that challenge. Michael Bracewell's scintillating cultural dissection of "Pop Life in Albion from Wilde to Goldie" concludes that in the mid 1970s "Sexuality itself was being manipulated in a way that England, looking on with fascinated ambivalence and primal hostility, had not seen since the trial of Oscar Wilde".[7] Wilde and Bowie were fused together in the anarchistic libertinism of Michael Moorcock's Jerry Cornelius Quartet. The novels came out between 1969 and 1977 and were probably the most audacious fiction being produced at the time. Most British "literary fiction" of the 1970s was too inert to engage with the political and cultural rebellion sweeping the country, preferring instead to dissect the introverted affairs of a disenchanted bourgeoisie or, if alert to wider social trends, to deride and satirise them (the best example being Malcolm Bradbury's 1975 *The History Man* which lampooned an unprincipled sociology lecturer who capitalised on leftish academic fashions for his own cynical ends). Authentic engagement and creative interplay tended to take place on the margins of literary respectability in a wild melange of sci-fi, satire, erotica and underground art.[8] Moorcock, who also wrote and played with Hawkwind and Blue Oyster Cult, was politically radical and excited by the shifting sands of the culture. Jerry Cornelius, a bisexual anti-authoritarian anarchist who battled the neo fascist Miss Brunner (based on Margaret Thatcher) across the parallel realities of the Multiverse, was a perfect reflection of the avant-garde of 1970s Britain.

Not unconnected to this cultural effervescence, radical social movements such as the Gay Liberation Front had began to develop in unexpected directions. In 1974 the GLF fragmented in to the London Lesbian and Gay Switchboard, *Gay News* and the Gay Marxist Front, which in turn became Gay Left, a collective and magazine of the same name. Gay Left ran from 1975 to 1980 and attempted to produce a Marxist explanation of gay oppression and how the struggle for homosexual rights was an integral part of the struggle for socialism. The magazine's contributors were a cross section of social and sexual campaigners such as the SWP's David Widgery, the radical feminist Bea Campbell and the social historian Jeffrey Weeks, who in 1977 produced with Sheila Rowbotham a ground breaking short book for Pluto Press: *Socialism and the New Life: The Personal and Sexual Politics of Edward Carpenter and Havelock Ellis.* The book grew out of talks at the LSE in 1974 and group discussions with gay and women workers at the Workers' Educational Association and the Essex Road Women's Centre. Rowbotham and Weeks examined their subjects in relation to "the political implications of women's control over their bodies; the separation of sexual pleasure from procreation; the significance of homosexual love, of free unions, of changed ways of life and the significance of all these to the labour and socialist movements", issues which "were now being discussed again on the left".[9]

Discussion led to action. In March 1974 a number of gay activists set up the South London Gay Community Centre at 78 Railston Rd, Brixton, to "come out into the clear light of day with a public statement of gay identity".[10] It was part of a new assertiveness in proclaiming that identity, demonstrated to dramatic perfection in John Hurt's portrayal of Quentin Crisp in the TV film *The Naked Civil Servant* (1975). The Gay Community Centre was a refuge but also a focus of collective debate, cooking, dancing, theatre and political campaigning. Established as a squat next door to the Women's' Centre and down the road from the Anarchist News Service, a Claimants Union, the Race Today Collective and a food co-operative, it stayed open until eventual eviction in April 1976, but even then it "became the nucleus for further political activity after the closure of the centre and grew, over time, as an experiment in new communal living arrange-ments".[11] Despite its modest size it was essential to plans for the first London Gay Pride March in 1976 and to forming alliances between gay rights and anti-racist activists in Brixton.

For a brief period in the mid 1970s there existed the tanta-lising possibility of real alliances between the political and cultural left in Britain. In April-May 1973 John Gorman, a printer, artist and union activist, created and presented an exhibition of trade union banners at the Whitechapel Gallery entitled "Banner Bright" (he later produced an Illustrated History). From 1973 to 1975 a project funded by the Greater London Arts Association allowed the socialist feminist artists Kay Hunt, Margaret Harrison and Mary Kelly to exhaustively record the experiences of female workers at the Metal Box factory in Southwark. After an exhibition of film, photos, text and graphics recorded the harsh work conditions and the unequal division of labour between male and female workers, the artists were banned from the factory. Work of this nature was sometimes supported and promoted by Artists for Democracy, an umbrella organisation of socialist artists active from 1974 to 1977. Set up in a large squat renamed the Fitzrovia Cultural Centre by the left wing artist David Medalla, AFD focused primarily on providing artistic support and materials to liberation struggles in Asia and Africa.

Unfortunately the potential of radical art to support Labour's ambition to effect a fundamental shift in wealth and power was soon aborted by the Labour government's repudiation of the socialist policies that had carried it to power. For despite the efforts of groups such as the IS/SWP and the squatters movement to create and sustain extra parliamentary activism that might offer an alternative to the "Labourism" so derided by socialist theorists like Ralph Miliband, and Benn's efforts to utilise the IWC to promote and extend workplace democracy in British industry, the central arena for challenging the political status quo in the UK remained a narrow and disadvantageous one – Whitehall and Parliament. The co-ordinated institutional resistance to Benn's White Paper had demonstrated exactly how disadvantageous. Nor did Benn and the left have a natural majority within the Parliamentary Labour Party (PLP) that it could ever have appealed to. Benn knew this, telling Foot in 1975, when both men were trying and failing to get the government to adopt more radical economic policies and Foot sought to blame Labour's tenuous Parliamentary majority, "It isn't because we haven't got a majority...it's because the Cabinet doesn't believe in the policy. If we had majority of a hundred we wouldn't implement it".[12]

Benn and the Labour left inside Parliament urgently needed a vibrant and sympathetic extra-Parliamentary adjunct and support, yet most of the non-Labour left was mired so deeply in a fixed model of revolutionary socialism that privileged the factory (seldom the office or the home) and the working class (seldom the progressive middle class) that they were, ironically, bereft of wider political perspective. A useful analysis by John McIlroy finds that as trade union militancy receded while unions waited to see what the Social Contract would deliver, the far left simply repeated itself to less and less effect. At a moment when the British political scene was at its most protean and unpredictable the ideological and strategic conceptions of the orthodox Marxist left were still driven by "workerism and economism" which "continued to alienate many women, black workers and those with a broader conception of politics".[13]

They would not find that broader conception of politics amongst the self-declared revolutionaries of the period. The IS/SWP had thrown itself into the dead-end of Factory Branches and Leading Areas, concepts conjured up by its intellectual guru Tony Cliff. Cliff and his acolytes ostensibly revered the working class "organic intellectual" (i.e. a proletarian who, unaided by themselves, had somehow found class consciousness and Marxist theory but now needed the direction of the Vanguard Party) but had little to no feel for the reality of working class life. The IS's National Organiser in the early 1970s, Jim Higgins, was a genuine working class intellectual with solid trade union experience whom Cliff sidelined and ignored once he threatened to bring the IS in to contact with the real world. After many disagreements with Cliff he left the IS and later characterised its approach to politics as "... a paradigm of the worst possible application of democratic centralism and a reductio ad absurdum of Lenin's politics".[14]

The most prominent British Marxist intellectuals, grouped around and writing for the *New Left Review* (NLR), were not dissimilar in attitude although they presented their ideas in a very different idiom. In a series of influential essays in the 1960s the NLR's leading lights Perry Anderson and Tom Nairn developed a thesis of Britain as a politically and culturally stagnant society that had never gone through a full blown Bourgeois Revolution, as in France. Lacking this decisive break with Feudalism Britain had therefore not developed healthy republican institutions, a militant labour movement or, on the academic plain, a "classical sociology" or "National Marxism" to function as an ideological corrective to an aristocratic/land owning/City based ruling class that still dominated British culture. This culture was therefore characterised by "moralistic vapouring" "paltry English empiricism", "the stony recesses of Trade Union conservatism", "the nullity of native intellectual traditions" and a "dilettante literary culture". In short, "a supine Bourgeoisie produced a subordinate Proletariat".[15]

There were interesting nuggets of truth here but they were obscured by an intense schematicism that weeded out complexities and inconvenient evidence in favour of "global theories of society, articulated in a totalising conceptual system".[16] In the 1970s Anderson produced two of the most dazzling works of Marxist "total history", *Passages from Antiquity to Feudalism* (1974) and *Lineages of the Absolutist State* (1976), which demonstrated both his immense intellectual range and detached perspective on individual lives. Anderson and Nairn's thesis was strongly attacked by a very different type of Marxist historian, E.P Thompson, author of *The Making of the English Working Class.* Thompson, criticised by Anderson/Nairn for "moralism" and "socialist populism", pointed out that "Minds which thirst for a tidy Platonism very quickly become impatient with actual history".[17] From a deep well of knowledge about British working class history he tore Anderson and Nairn's "totalising conceptual system" to pieces by reinserting those who did not neatly fit within it – Lollards, Levellers, Chartists, syndicalists, ethical socialists and Communists – and insisting that Revolution and systemic change seldom occurred in one momentous event but over time and with great complexity. He slated the idea that Britain, the first industrial power and the touchstone of Marx and Engels' work, had not fully developed capitalism and that it lacked a vigorous working class movement in comparison to countries such as France, Italy and Germany (whose National Marxisms had done so much to avoid the triumph of Fascism).

The inevitable offshoot of the Anderson/Nairn thesis was a disregard and contempt for the British working class and trade union movement. It led to an arrogant assumption of command and leadership, in that "A political science capable of guiding the working class to final victory can only be born within a general intellectual matrix which challenges bourgeois ideology in every sector of thought and represents a decisive, hegemonic alternative to the status quo".[18] In one sense this was obvious although not very helpful to actual struggles. In another it meant that no individual challenge to capitalist relations of production – because by definition it could never be a decisive, hegemonic alternative to the status quo – could ever be significant, at least not without a "general intellectual matrix" conceived and delivered by the academics and intellectuals of the NLR.

Both the IS/SWP and the NLR patronised and insulted British workers who failed to achieve what they considered the correct level of awareness of their position within the capitalist system.[19] And yet Anderson and Nairn had identified, in convoluted fashion, a real political problem. In his *Considerations on Western Marxism* (1976) Anderson succinctly categorised the central insight of the Italian Marxist Antonio Gramsci as the challenge to socialists of capitalist cultural "hegemony", i.e. "... this hegemonic system of power was defined by the degree of consent it obtained from the popular masses which it dominated, and a consequent reduction in the scale of coercion needed to repress them".[20] In light of this, it was clearly essential that a mass socialist movement appeal to the working class in a language and style that spoke to their lives and stripped away the cultural/linguistic/legal camouflage of a society built on inequalities of wealth, power and opportunity. Anderson also pinpointed the central weakness of "Western Marxism" (by which he meant the corpus of theoretical writing produced by philosophers such as Adorno, Marcuse, Sartre, Della Volpe and Althusser) in that unlike Gramsci its major theorists advanced purely "speculative constructions ... a priori conceptual schemes ... not necessarily inconsistent with empirical evidence, but always undemonstrated by it in their mode of presentation".[21] This was a polite way of saying that they reduced Marxism, a great explanatory and subversive doctrine used as a clarion cry of liberation by revolutionaries such as James Connolly and Che Guevara, to dry abstractions characterised by circular logic and impenetrable academic jargon.

With some exceptions the IS/SWP and the NLR existed in their own self-created realities. In so doing they missed entirely the organic intellectuals and counter-hegemonic forces that were in front of them all along, fighting within trade unions and the Labour Party, on rent strikes and occupations, working in the NHS and in workers co-operatives, and living in squats, communes and council estates. In the 1970s these activists and campaigners were challenging capitalism in numerous original and courageous ways. And they did so without the guidance or approval of political and intellectual vanguards.

Chapter Nine

Useful Work v. Useless Toil

The Labour government had reached an impasse. To have any chance of governing effectively it needed a clear Parliamentary majority. This left Wilson little choice but to call another General Election in October 1974. With the possibility that Labour might secure a solid majority and the left of the Party might then attempt to implement Labour's manifesto in its entirety, the October General Election was conducted in an acrimonious and hysterical atmosphere. More rumours of right-wing paramilitaries bubbled to the service. Hypothetical military coups were discussed at Sandhurst where Brian Crozier addressed two hundred assembled junior officers and told them that if a left-wing government went too far the Army would have to intervene. Reportedly the officers "rose as one and applauded for five minutes".[1] As the chief spokesman of the left Benn was always under heavy attack, but the Tory supporting press never got the chance to unleash its biggest slanders because the printers trade union NATSOPA refused to print the most extreme anti-Labour smear stories prepared by the *Daily Express* and *Daily Mail*.[2] A decade later, under Thatcher, the print unions would pay a heavy price for standing in the way of the right-wing media's political agenda.

Media coverage of the General Election displayed an astonishing level of anti-Labour bias. The BBC scheduled parts one and two of a ludicrously unbalanced *Panorama* programme on Benn, which amongst other things questioned his sanity, to bookend Labour's main TV Party Political Broadcast. Despite this onslaught Labour increased its overall share of the vote by 2% and now secured a Parliamentary majority, albeit a very slim one of three. But even though Labour had gone to the electorate twice in one year on a radical reforming programme and had now secured a majority with, arguably, a mandate to carry it out, Benn's political strength was beginning to erode. The cumulative effect of unrelenting media attack and character assassination had damaged his standing and support within the party. For Wilson, Benn was now a political and PR nightmare. For Benn, Wilson was a straw man with no political vision at all. "That man is capable of being Prime Minister four times without doing anything to change the structure of power in society" he noted bitterly in his diary straight after the election.[3]

It was made crystal clear to Wilson and Benn immediately after the General Election what the representatives of business wanted. On 12th October the *Economist* demanded Benn's removal as Secretary of State for Industry. On 16th October the *Financial Times* reported that the Director General of the CBI had told the Prime Minister that "there was absolutely no room for compromise or negotiation about further state intervention in industry or further nationalisation".[4] The CBI undoubtedly reflected the views of the business and City elite it represented. A breakdown of the voting intentions of 200 senior City figures in the October General Election carried out by *Investors Review* found that of those polled 73% would vote Conservative, 18% Liberal, and 9% were undecided. None of them said they would vote Labour.[5]

The CBI and its jittery media mouthpieces could have saved themselves much worry. By the end of 1974 Benn had effectively already lost the battle to make the Industry Act a powerful instrument to redirect British industrial policy. He had run up against a wall of incredulity and opposition within his department most of whose senior officials did not even seem to understand what he meant when he discussed Labour policy. Shortly after the October election Sir Anthony Part brought the concerns of those officials directly to Benn, reporting that they were "shocked" to hear that Benn considered that the planning agreements central to the industrial strategy could be extended from collective bargaining on terms and conditions to bargaining for power *within* industry, thereby threatening management's prerogative to manage. "I'm sorry", replied Benn, "but what did you think the fundamental and irreversible shift in the balance of wealth and power was about if it wasn't this?".[6]

At the Treasury Healey had already moved away from his brief dalliance with threats of radical redistributive taxation and investing for growth. On 30th October he submitted a Memorandum entitled "Public Expenditure Priorities" to the Cabinet that reported back on an earlier decision in September to limit the growth of public expenditure to an average of 2¾% up to 1978-79, and to consider priorities within that envelope. Ominously he reported that "Giving a high priority to particular programmes or services does not mean that spending on them may increase without limit or restraint". In that spirit he considered that there was "a pressing need to phase out the very heavy subsidies at present paid to hold nationalised industry prices down, and more gradually to reduce the cost of food subsidies. The scope for improving less urgent social security benefits will be restricted in the next few years; and it is necessary to ensure that the costs of a larger housing programme are fairly shared between tenants and taxpayers".[7] This was in complete contradiction to the promised fundamental and irreversible shift in the balance of wealth and power, about which the senior civil service made its views clear in a memorandum to Healey from the Treasury's Permanent Secretary copied to the Governor of the Bank of England. It told the Chancellor that "current policies were unworkable and there was no longer support for them at official level in the Treasury".[8] Healey seems to have let pass the neutral civil service informing the elected government that it did not support its policies, probably because by this time he did not support them himself. At the time this was a relatively gentle introduction to the monetarist thinking now infecting the Treasury. The pain would increase as the knife cut deeper.

Benn, though, was now increasingly diverting his attention and energies from the industrial policy to campaigning for a "No" vote in the forthcoming referendum on UK membership of the European Economic Community (EEC), which Wilson had only agreed to as a safety valve for the deep divisions on the issue within the party. Although Benn saw the issue as vital to the industrial policy (for under the terms of the 1957 Treaty of Rome EEC rules might cut across and forbid the interventionist state support so central to the policy) it was arguably a mistake to fight two such battles at the same time, especially as failure in one (the referendum) would provide Wilson the excuse he needed to sideline him permanently. Benn sensed the shifting sands in Cabinet and that despite the passing of the White Paper it was by no means certain that even the diluted form of the industrial strategy would make it on to the statute book. In November he acknowledged in the privacy of his diary that in order to achieve any of his goals "I am going to have to build up massive support now through major speeches". Reaching out beyond Parliament was his only realistic strategy as in his view "There is a systematic social democratic betrayal of socialist policy, and the Cabinet has nothing in common with the aspirations of the movement".[9] Yet even though it was now clear the Industry Act would be much less comprehensive that Benn had wanted the security services continued to regard him as a serious threat to the continuation of the UK's capitalist system and the privileges of its political and business class. For the Act was not the only battle-front. There was still industrial democracy.

The most emblematic struggle on the use of public funds to support new, experimental ways to run companies and provide goods and services arose from Benn's idea for an "Alternative Corporate Plan" to be drawn up by the Shop Stewards Combine Committee at Lucas Aerospace, a unique cross-plant, multi-union structure that represented 13,000 staff and shop floor workers in seventeen LA factories. The workers on the Combine Committee were an example of how politically conscious trade union representatives had become in the 1970s. Between 1970 and 1974 LA had cut 5,000 jobs from its workforce and in its battles with the employer the Committee had developed in militancy and self-confidence. It did not trust the management to safeguard the company or run it efficiently, and as soon as Labour was elected in February 1974 it began to press the government to include LA in its nationalisation plans. They shared many of the IWC's reservations about traditional nationalisation and were looking for a more democratic model of public ownership but they believed that LA's future was better safeguarded in public than private hands. As the earliest and still definitive work on the Lucas Aerospace Combine put it, "the battle lines would be clearer, the arguments for alternative work in place of redundancy would be stronger, and the possibility of appealing to the needs of the wider community would be greater".[10]

In November 1974 the Combine asked Benn if it could put a case to him to include LA in Labour's plans to nationalise the aircraft industry. Over the strident objections of his officials Benn held a meeting with thirty four of the Combine's shop stewards in his large DoI office which he felt was "one of the most inspiring meetings I have ever attended".[11] Although he "found myself wholly in sympathy with them" he had to tell them that he lacked the authority to nationalise LA. Such a decision would have to go through the Cabinet and Benn knew he could never persuade his colleagues to extend the already reduced nationalisation plans. Instead he suggested that the Combine produce an "Alternative Corporate Plan" for the company and bring that back to Industry as the basis for LA's involvement in an NEB sponsored Planning Agreement. The Combine set to work on the Alternative Plan, which would have repercussions well beyond Benn's time in office.

In January 1975 the representatives took Benn's suggestion back to a full meeting of the Combine which considered if it should press for full nationalisation through the usual channels, or develop its own plan based on transforming LA's productive capacity from military hardware to a full range of innovative and socially useful products. There was massive enthusiasm for the more radical and creative alternative and the Combine went out to all of LA's factories to gather ideas and concepts for inclusion in the ACP. Suggestions and blueprints flooded in from a workforce never before asked to bring its own ideas to the table. The Combine considered them all and settled on five separate categories for proposed alternative production – medical equipment such as portable kidney machines and "designs for the disabled"; alternative energy technologies such as solar cells and wind turbines for more ecological storage and conversion; new transport solutions such as rail-road vehicles and airships; revolutionary breaking systems utilising electro-magnetism; and innovatory underseas remote controlled exploratory devices.

In many ways the ordinary workers at LA were setting out a progressive green agenda that was decades ahead of its time. The ACP proposed "production processes that that would tend to conserve and recycle energy, and would liberate rather than suppress human creativity".[12] Although few thought of it in explicitly socialist terms it was in embryo William Morris's "factory as it might be" – a place of work where workers utilised their innate creativity to increase their own job satisfaction and to benefit society rather than a corporate balance sheet, the very application of "useful work versus useless toil".[13] The logic of the Alternative Corporate Plan was profoundly anti-capitalist and if widely implemented would pose a fundamental threat to British managements' right to manage. Benn had no problem with that, in fact he encouraged it.

But in pushing for a plan for Lucas Aerospace generated from the workers themselves, and through his use of the Department of Industry budget to help establish workers' co-operatives, he had crossed a very definite line. Secure in the knowledge that Benn was politically isolated at Cabinet level Sir Anthony Part now "declared war" on his Secretary of State.[14]

Chapter Ten

Alternative Economic Strategy

As Permanent Secretary, Part was also the DoI's Accounting Officer with responsibility to "sign off" the department's annual accounts to Parliament's Public Accounts Committee. This was usually not contentious and went through as a matter of routine but shortly before the October 1974 General Election Part informed Benn that he was considering submitting to him an Accounting Officer's Minute, an arcane and seldom used procedure which a) asked for his specific authorisation for certain controversial items of expenditure (in this case the funding of the workers' co-ops) and b) implied that the allocation of that funding was in some form improper or financially imprudent. Part did not at that time follow through, but the threat remained. In January 1975, when Benn not only did not desist from this programme but stepped it up (the last straw for Part may have been Benn's hosting of over thirty workers from the Lucas Aerospace Combine in his office and his public support for their grass roots initiatives) Part carried out his threat.

As soon as it became known that he had done so Wilson asked for clarification. Part wrote to the Prime Minister providing his reasons. Benn immediately summoned him to his office and told him that he intended to challenge every aspect of Part's note. He reminded Part that every case cited had been discussed and signed off by the full Cabinet and that no such Minute had ever been submitted on other expenditure, only on these relatively small amounts allocated to groups of workers. Benn finished by telling Part bluntly that in his view Part's Minute had been "a matter of political judgment, not financial propriety" and he intended to make that case to the Prime Minister.[1] Faced with this uncompromising resistance Part tried to soften Benn's report to

Wilson. He was particularly concerned to refute Benn's accusation that the Whitehall machine and the use to which it put procedures like the Accounting Officer's Minute was conditioned by the social and political bias of senior officials. "I cannot accept that any civil servant is political" he stressed. Benn simply replied that to him that was not a term of abuse.

Faced with Benn's challenge not only to the note but also to the civil service's claim to political neutrality Part backtracked. The simmering argument between Secretary of State and Permanent Secretary was deflated a few weeks later when Part suffered a mild heart attack (characteristically, Benn made a friendly visit to him in the hospital). The many attacks, delays and procedural obstructions that DoI officials flung at Benn throughout his time in office wrought a fundamental change of attitude in a man who had to this point worked smoothly and well within the Whitehall machine (as Minister for Technology in the 1966-70 Labour government he had not encountered major obstruction). By 1974, though, Benn had shifted politically to the left and had a firmer commitment to the socialist aspirations of the wider party and its programme as outlined in the General Election manifestos. In February 1975, when considering the senior mandarins of the civil service, he concluded "I don't think anyone can beat them. I have been awfully slow to see it, but the only way you can make sense of any of these problems is by realising that the civil service is defending the class interests of owners and professional people ...".[2] Benn now perceived that the civil service – especially the Treasury, Cabinet Office and the FCO, whose senior officials had risen swiftly through an exclusive "Fast Stream" cadre most of whom were vetted Oxbridge graduates – would inevitably provide Labour ministers with intellectual analysis and policy options reflecting the world view of a socially conservative ruling elite. It was because of this that he set out a deliberate and challenging "Alternative Economic Strategy" which drew from Labour's

Programme 1973 and the policy work that went into it.

On February 25th 1975 Benn presented a paper, which he had drafted with the help of his economics advisor Francis Cripps, titled "A Choice of Economic Policies" to the Cabinet's Ministerial Committee on Economic Strategy. In it he offered up two options. Strategy A was a perfect prediction of what would become the government's economic strategy for the next four years – pay restraint, public spending cuts, tax increases, deflation and consequently "the withdrawal of support for the government by the TUC and labour movement". Strategy B was in essence the "Alternative Economic Strategy" that the Labour left would develop and promote for the next ten years as an alternative to both monetarism and Keynesianism. Benn argued that as well as an alternative approach to the economic policy advocated by Healey there was an urgent need for "A full explanation by the government to the nation of the reasons for the crisis – that is to say, it is a world slump related to a failure to invest, not just the fault of the unions". His paper recommended selective import restrictions, increased assistance to industry to safeguard employment and encourage investment, egalitarian and progressive taxation measures, saving of foreign exchange by substantial cuts in defence spending, control of capital outflows, and government control of the banks and other financial institutions to assist the programmes of the National Enterprise Board.[3]

Benn's paper was the tip of an iceberg. From 1973 to 1983 the AES defined the Labour left's economic policy. It had a broad spectrum of support across the labour and trade union movement and at different times there were more, or less, radical versions of it. At the democratic socialist end of the spectrum were Marxist economists such as Bob Rowthorn, the IWC, the organised Labour left including the CP, and Tony Benn. At the liberal Keynesian end of the spectrum were economists from the Cambridge Economic Policy Group led by Nicholas Kaldor (who advised the Treasury during the Wilson governments of the 1960s and again in the 1970s), Wynne Godley and Francis Cripps.[4] Earlier versions of the AES were not as fleshed out as later ones, but at its core it argued for reflation of the economy to raise output and create employment, price and import controls to protect British industry and prevent it from exploiting that protection, compulsory planning agreements to achieve better investment and production flows, public ownership of the major financial institutions to control the City and to use pension funds for positive ends, a severe reduction in military expenditure and an attack on systemic inequality through progressive taxation and social spending. It was not, by definition, a strategy for the "instant socialism" demanded by the revolutionary left but if implemented it would undoubtedly lead to "a radical shift in the balance of power in favour of the working class and its allies".[5]

The AES received some solid intellectual support from the work of the Cambridge economists around Kaldor, who had been pushing Wilson for more flexible economic policies since the 1960s. Kaldor had been a major player in British and international economic theory since his "A Model of Economic Growth" in 1957 suggested that savings and investment and thus growth could be stimulated by "endogenous factors" (i.e. spending power, which could be increased by public investment and other policy interventions by government) and not solely "exogenous factors" (i.e. technical invention, entrepreneurial input etc) that naturally appeared if left to the free market.[6] The theory was an evidence base for Keynesian growth models and as such of great interest to societies struggling to achieve economic take off. His conclusions on growth and the factors that stimulated or retarded it later led him to adopt a critical stance towards the IMF and to advocate a range of protective measures for infant industries such as export subsidies and import duties. Initially he proposed these for industrialising countries such as India but he came to believe they would be suitable for Britain too. Driven by this analysis the Cambridge Economic Policy Group offered solutions to capital flight and inflation centred on import controls, experimental dual exchange rates (one for trade and one for capital, with the tighter capital rate designed to restrict the ability of City speculators to cripple trade) and increased progressive taxation.

Their work, empirical and rigorous yet unashamedly redistributive, was added to and enriched by a group of Marxist economists also based at Cambridge such as Bob Rowthorn, who had written for *Black Dwarf* in the 1960s. This latter group, unlike Kaldor's, which fed in straight to Whitehall and Chancellor Healey, worked closely with the IWC. Together they produced in 1974 a pamphlet written explicitly to buttress and support Benn's industrial strategy. *An Alternative Economic Strategy for the Labour Movement* was aimed at activists within the trade union movement, and it advocated a democratically controlled economy based on participatory social production. Unfortunately for those struggling to develop a viable alternative to creeping monetarism the lack of a wider education programme within the unions to propagandise for the industrial strategy meant that it was often taken for granted or simply not understood. The imbalance of research and statistical modelling resources between left and right was enormous, with Healey and Wilson fed analysis and statistics directly from the Treasury whilst "... Jones and Scanlon were dependent on advice from the TUC Economic Department, itself heavily influenced by changing Treasury thinking".[7]

Although much more work would be done on the AES later in the decade and once Labour was in opposition in the early 1980s, inside the 1974-79 Labour government it was never given the opportunity to breathe and develop. After a long debate Wilson responded that Benn's analysis "oversimplified to the point of distortion" and dismissed it as a feasible alternative. It appears that Wilson engaged in his own oversimplification in his haste to dismiss the thinking of a man who had gone from being one of his friends and confidantes in the 1960s to his most hated political enemy in the 1970s. This animus was demonstrated in March 1975 when Benn submitted another memorandum to Wilson in response to Healey's request to Cabinet that the government adjust the terms of the Social Contract with the TUC, specifically that TUC guidelines to its constituent unions on pay restraint were not tight enough, thus threatening, as he saw it, the attack on inflation. Benn disagreed, writing "The strategy proposed by the Chancellor is bound to be seen by the Labour movement and the whole country as a policy of despair, representing an admission of failure of our economic policy". Benn suggested policies drawn from the AES such as deep cuts in defence spending allied to import quotas, higher tariffs and targeted subsidies to industry in exchange for price control. When given the paper Wilson wrote a short note in red ink for his office across the cover "I haven't read it, don't propose to, but I disagree with it".[8]

Benn came away from such collisions with a depressing realisation of how far he now was from most of his Cabinet colleagues. Although his economic prescriptions at that time were not radically different from highly respectable economists such as Kaldor, his alliance with the IWC, his support for workers at Lucas and Meriden and his efforts to achieve a comprehensive Industry Act had alienated him from politicians who, if they had a political vision at all, were content to replay the politics of the 1950s and had little to no understanding of social movements or intellectual trends on the left. For them Benn was a romantic and a poser. Even those who had supported him felt he was cracking under the strain of a monumental campaign of personal vilification in the media. When he told Michael Foot that he suspected his phone was being tapped by the security services (as it was) Foot responded "Tony, you're going nuts".[9]

But others saw things differently. In their analysis of the

Labour New Left of the 1970s Panitch and Leys identify the nature of Benn's threat to the political establishment, most especially to Labour's traditionally right-wing social democratic leadership, in that his refusal to cease advocating socialist policies within government "... helped focus the party's attention on what might be done if Labour had a leadership less deferential in the face of bureaucratic statism and more committed to mobilising popular support for socialist policies".[10] MI5 saw this, even if the rather naive Foot did not. In early 1975 it tightened the noose around Benn. Dorril and Ramsey's exhaustive and definitive work on the unsanctioned and frequently illegal activities of MI5 in the 1960s and 1970s (and its links to the political and paramilitary far right) uncovered a massive covert operation centred on the Secretary of State for Industry. "Benn's telephones were tapped, his house was bugged and he was under open surveillance".[11] In clear view of journalists camped permanently outside his house, his domestic refuse was daily taken away by a man in an expensive Jaguar car. He and his family received regular death threats.

It was not only Benn who was carefully watched. Judith Hart, the Minister for Overseas Development, was also under constant surveillance. For many years MI5 had harboured a deep distrust of Hart based on a combination of her politics and a misidentification of her with a woman of a similar name with some Eastern Bloc connections. The misidentification would have been obvious to those who bothered to investigate a little further, which MI5 did not because the attribution of Communist sympathies was a convenient accusation against a left-wing Labour minister. In 1973, when Hart tried to telephone friends in Chile after the coup to determine if they were alive and unharmed, MI5 recorded her calls and added them to the file as evidence of her Marxist sympathies and connections. It also produced transcripts of a few phone calls she had made to Communist Party HQ in King St to discuss solidarity actions with socialists abroad. When she was made Minister for Overseas Development MI5 began to drip feed this mixture of half-truths and exaggeration to Wilson, and MI6 Chief Maurice Oldfield suggested to the Prime Minister that she be denied sight of certain foreign policy documents. As a result Wilson considered removing her from her position. Although he retained her she was forbidden to travel abroad, an extraordinary and very public mark of distrust by the Foreign Policy establishment and her own party leader.[12]

The presence of socialists like Hart, Benn and Heffer at ministerial level had driven MI5 to step up surveillance of those in the wider political and trade union world who might be labelled their allies. Ken Coates was subject to routine surveillance although he had not broken any laws nor advocated doing so. MI5's Section F1A widened its net of phone tapping and other monitoring to include trade union officials and activists who were in no conceivable manner engaged in "subversive" activities. In early 1975 F1A expanded its surveillance of the Militant Tendency (a relatively small Trotskyist group that sought to join and influence local Labour Party Branches and had some influence in the Labour Party Young Socialists) to include any members of the Labour Party who were "in touch" with Militant activists and sometimes agreed or voted with them, or any that its sources deemed "ultra left" – in effect any members who advocated Labour Party policy as laid out in the 1974 Manifesto. MI5 was especially exercised by the activities of the Campaign for Labour Party Democracy (CLPD) which had been formed in 1973 to give ordinary members more say in decision making, one crucial element of which was ensuring that MPs could be deselected by their local parties if they did not measure up or if they refused to advocate party policy. F1A focused heavily on constituencies where it was suspected that "left-wing activists were attempting to remove right-wing Labour MPs"[13] even though this was entirely legitimate activity within Labour Party rules.

Media hysteria notwithstanding, the existence of a few Trotskyist activists in local Labour Party Branches did not cause seasoned MI5 and Whitehall officials sleepless nights. Of much more concern was the existence of socialists in ministerial office who reflected the views and wishes of those Branches. In January 1975 the DoI Minister Michael Meacher wrote in a newspaper article of "the anarchy of capitalist markets" and called for their firmer regulation in order to save jobs and secure investment. Sir Anthony Part complained to Benn that such language was inappropriate for a government minister as it was a "political phrase". When Benn told him that he had approved the article himself and that it reflected Labour Party policy, Part coldly replied "I wanted to warn you".[14]

Warnings were issued elsewhere throughout the spring of 1975 but usually to only rhetorical effect. In April Len Murray, the usually placid General Secretary of the TUC, had called the Stock Exchange "a relic of the 19th century" that was "no longer relevant to the needs of British industry".[15] In the same month Benn confirmed that the government intended to proceed with plans to set up a National Enterprise Board and that pensions and insurance funds would have to invest in the NEB (and other publicly owned enterprises) a minimum amount of their new funds. This was simply Labour policy as outlined by NEC Home Policy Committee papers, the 1973 Programme and the 1974 election manifestos. It could have been driven through even more effectively if the government had legislated on the TUC's policy of having 50% trade union representation on the boards of pension funds, something not at all unusual in Scandinavian countries but a radical challenge to the great financial institutions of the UK.

For the CBI and the City, worse was to follow. On May 7th the National Economic Development Council (the famous "Neddy", created by Harold MacMillan in 1962) agreed to set up a committee to keep external finance for industrial investment under permanent review. Another media assault on Benn followed only this time it was overshadowed by a far more orchestrated attack on him for his leadership of the campaign for a "No" vote to continued membership of the EEC in the Referendum due to take place in June. In many ways the Referendum – the first ever held throughout the entire UK – was Benn's creation. He had been the driving force behind the Labour NEC and Shadow Cabinet's rejection of the terms of entry negotiated by Heath, and strongly supported Labour Conference policy that if elected a Labour government would renegotiate those terms and then put them to the nation in a Referendum on continued membership. That policy had been a key part of Labour's General Election Manifesto and could hardly be ignored, even by Wilson.

If a majority voted "No" the UK would exit the EEC. Benn saw this as essential to the success of the Alternative Economic Strategy. In his view the EEC restricted the ability of a Member State to develop national economic policy beyond a strictly capitalist framework, specifically that its "anti-competition" clauses narrowed and in some cases disallowed the kind of public investment and intervention in industry that was the core of Labour's industrial strategy. As if to confirm his worst fears, in January 1975 Benn was told that the Foreign Office would block the Industry Bill in the Legislation Committee of the House if he did not give a pledge that it would conform to Rome Treaty obligations. At the time he had successfully resisted this but it reinforced his suspicion of the Treaty and the institutions it had birthed. He would now stake everything on leading a campaign for UK withdrawal from the EEC.

Chapter Eleven

Commitments with the City

For the British left in the 1970s "Europe" was increasingly a major problem. After the formation of the European Coal and Steel Community in 1952 it was clear that a European Union of some kind would eventually emerge. The 1957 Treaty of Rome, signed by West Germany, France, Italy, the Netherlands, Belgium and Luxembourg, created the EEC and its core institutional structures – the European Commission, ultimately answerable to a Council of Heads of State, but still the creator and driver of European policy initiatives; the European Court of Justice (ECJ), which ruled on the lawful application of those policies; and the European Parliament, which in the 1970s had no law making capacity and was in effect a toothless focus group. For Benn and most of the left there were two "original sins" at the heart of this process. Firstly, the anti-democracy of the Commission/Parliament relationship which gave legislative initiative to the unelected officials of the Commission and sidelined Members of the European Parliament. Secondly, the identification of trade liberalisation as the primary raison d'etre of the EEC gave the entire European project a negative rather than a positive thrust. The new institutions, for all their cross-European imagery and potential, were only really authorised to remove perceived obstacles to trade and competition. The prospect of the EEC developing pan-European social and labour market policies had been considered and rejected at its inception.[1]

By the time Labour began to draw up new policy on the EEC in response to British entry in 1973 it was clear that either the terms of UK membership had to be amended to allow Labour to pursue its full industrial and economic strategy or a Labour government would have to withdraw entirely. Only in the 1980s did the left begin to reassess the EEC (later the EU) in the light of the "Social Europe" model, i.e. formal consultation mechanisms between the "social partners" within European institutions, plus Qualified Majority Voting in the EU Council that led to progressive employment legislation and stricter health & safety standards. Crucially, the pro-worker component of what in the 1970s was still known as the "Common Market" emerged not from EEC institutions themselves but from the nation states of Scandinavia and Northern Europe (the UK excepted). It was not until 1996 that many of these elements were codified by Jacques Delors in the European Social Charter as fundamental social rights which he regarded as essential if European economic and monetary union was to bridge the "democratic deficit" and contain a progressive social dimension.[2]

The Social Charter was in the future and is now, following ratification of the neo-liberal Lisbon Treaty in 2009 and a series of pro-employer legal judgements by the ECJ that undermine collective bargaining rights, receding into the past. In 1974 Wilson had instructed Foreign Secretary Jim Callaghan to secure new terms of British membership. As neither Wilson nor Callaghan was very concerned about EEC rules preventing Labour carrying out a full bodied interventionist industrial strategy the attempt was half hearted at best. When the renegotiated terms were revealed it was quickly apparent that they had altered very little. On March 18th 1975 the Cabinet held an exhaustive debate on the new terms and on what the government's position regarding them should be. Benn made clear what he saw as the nub of the issue, claiming that "In practice, Britain will be governed by a European coalition government that we cannot change, dedicated to a capitalist or market economy theology".[3] Seven Cabinet members (Benn, Foot, Shore, Castle, Varley, Silkin and Ross) dissented from the majority's acceptance of the new terms. Given the importance of the issue and the seniority of the dissenters Wilson had little option but to suspend the usual practice of collective Cabinet responsibility for government decisions and allow them to campaign in their personal capacities for a No vote in the forthcoming Referendum.

Even so he issued guidelines that strictly limited this "dissent" to the Referendum campaign only, did not allow ministers to debate against each other publicly, to sit on platforms with representatives of the other parties, or to speak out against the renegotiated terms in the House. The restrictions were useful in muzzling or punishing inveterate rebels like Eric Heffer. On April 9th Heffer, ignoring Wilson's guidelines, made a blistering speech in the House against continued EEC membership. Wilson sacked him immediately. Later in the campaign Roy Jenkins and Shirley Williams would share platforms with Ted Heath without reproach from Wilson.

The split in the Labour Party on the EEC had nothing to do with attitudes to Europe as a cultural entity (Michael Foot appreciated Italian wine and the beauties of Venice as much as Roy Jenkins). It was an offshoot of a fundamental cleavage between a right-wing that wanted to yoke British capitalism to a pan-European bloc regardless of the EEC's democratic deficit, and a left-wing that wanted to retain the freedom to implement policies including capital and import controls that were not allowed under EEC rules. The battle over the terms of the treaty and membership itself was reflective of this divide, with Wilson, Healey, Jenkins and a majority of Conservatives and Liberals keen to support the Treaty and membership precisely because it was an institutional and legal fetter on future socialist policies. Hence, although a special Labour Party conference on the issue voted two to one in favour of a No vote, Wilson insisted that Labour Party funds and resources not be used to support the No campaign. Without that support the pro-EEC campaign had vastly more money and resources at its disposal.

In April the main clearing banks agreed to fund the "Britain in

Europe" campaign to the tune of £200,000. With the single exception of the *Morning Star* all British newspapers were unanimously behind a Yes vote. While the No campaign struggled with limited funding the leaders of the Yes campaign (Conservatives like Heath and Douglas Hurd, the Liberal leader Jeremy Thorpe and Labour pro-marketeers Roy Jenkins and Bill Rodgers) enjoyed meeting in secret for planning breakfasts at the Dorchester hotel in Mayfair, courtesy of its owner and future Tory party Treasurer Lord McAlpine. Rodgers later confessed how much more he enjoyed the superb fare provided for him at the Dorchester to that on offer in the "draughty halls" of the Labour and trade union movement.[4]

It was therefore not surprising that the result, announced on Thursday 5th June, was 17,378,581 (67.2 %) for Yes, and 8,470,073 (32%) for No. Given that Benn had been the prime mover for holding a Referendum and in the campaign for a No vote, the result was a severe political blow to him and his entire political project. Immediately his enemies scented blood. As rumours flew around Westminster and the media that Wilson would now sack Benn from Industry, Jack Jones – hitherto not very supportive of Benn's efforts to extend the powers of the Industry Act and to introduce workplace democracy, preferring to work on the Social Contract with Michael Foot – made a public statement that the unions had "a very great deal of confidence" in Benn and that to remove him from Industry would be an insult to them. Foot himself lobbied Wilson to retain Benn and many local Labour Party branches sent messages of support for him to Labour HQ in Woolworth Rd.

It was too late. The wheels were already in motion. On the morning of Monday 9th June the *Times* reported new proposals from Labour's Home Policy Committee, which Benn chaired to nationalise the clearing banks and to put their holdings at the disposal of the nation. The CBI made it clear they were vehemently hostile to this proposal and to Benn's continuance as

Industry Secretary. Sir Kenneth Keith, an aggressive corporate raider and Chairman of Hill Samuel Bank and Rolls Royce, told the *World at One* TV news programme that the plans would be "the end of the City of London as we know it today". The story had clearly been worked up over the weekend by Benn's enemies inside and outside government to add to the pressure on Wilson to remove him from what was still a vital and influential Cabinet post. The pressure was effective. Later in the day Benn received a message that Wilson wanted to see him at 6.00pm that evening. When he arrived at 10 Downing St he was shown straight into the Prime Minister who told him without any preamble that he wanted to move him from Industry to the Department of Energy.

Although still a Cabinet post Energy was nowhere near as central to the pursuance of the Alternative Economic Strategy as Industry and moving Benn from one to the other after fifteen months at Industry was a clear rebuke and demotion. Wilson insisted Benn tell him if he would accept that move within two hours. Benn played for time and said he could not give him an answer that night. He consulted his wife and family and political allies about his choice – either to resign completely and take the fight for Labour's socialist policies to the backbenches or to swallow his demotion to Energy and use his Cabinet position as best he could. Whilst many of his extra-Parliamentary allies felt he should resign and thus be free to speak out on all subjects as he liked, Foot, Jones and Scanlon urged him to stay in the Cabinet and ensure the Social Contract delivered. Late in the night after hours of urgent discussion Eric Varley, who was personally close to Wilson, phoned Benn and asked him to come to his office. Upon arrival he told Benn "I think Harold has entered in to commitments with the City or somebody, and he has to get rid of you".[5]

Despite Wilson's pressure for an answer the matter dragged late in to the next day Tuesday 10th June. Again summoned to Wilson, Benn arrived to be immediately asked "What is your answer?" whereupon the Prime Minister and his Industry Secretary had a blazing row. Benn said that his main concern remained the implementation of the Labour manifesto. Wilson insisted that he was as committed to that as Benn was. Benn said he did not accept this and accused Wilson of capitulating to pressure from the City and the media. "If you think this is going to save you you've made a great mistake" he told an angry Wilson, "they'll be pleased for twenty four hours and then they'll turn on you". Wilson said that he expected that to happen anyway and he had to have Benn's answer there and then. Benn told him that with great reluctance he would move to Energy and with that he walked out, slamming the door of the Prime Minister's office behind him.[6]

Although the media presented Benn's removal from Industry as a consequence of the Referendum result, this was never credible. Other Ministers such as Foot had been just as active in the No campaign as Benn and yet they retained their positions (indeed, the No vote campaigner Eric Varley was moved *into* Industry). In reality Benn's demotion "had everything to do with the way the centre-right of the Cabinet, the senior civil service and business circles saw Benn's socialist commitment"[7] and the threat that commitment posed to the vested interests of the British ruling class. After the Referendum result and Benn's removal from Industry the City brokers Simon and Coates declared that their "worst fear" of a "siege economy" could be put at rest, and it allowed that Chancellor Healey "now has two or three months grace to work out his counter-inflationary policy".[8] Desperately seeking to reassure them, Healey's close ally Edmund Dell used a written Parliamentary answer to confirm that despite the proposals of Labour's Home Policy Committee the government had no intention of nationalising the clearing banks.

One of Benn's closest trade union allies, Clive Jenkins, General Secretary of the Association of Scientific, Technical and

Managerial Staffs (ASTMS), was far less inclined to bow to the City's views on economic policy. In the run up to the Referendum he had made a strong case for the NEB and for direct intervention by government in the planning of investment flows, saying that "... the short term outlook of City decision making is incompatible with the need to restructure our economy for stable long-term growth...the City shows a wariness to lend to industry and a proclivity for those areas the City does understand – the property and short term money markets".[9] Jenkins had touched a nerve. In publicly criticising the City's historic under-investment in industry and the resultant liquidity crisis Benn and his allies had attacked the fundamental values of British finance. Not for nothing did the City record a zero vote for Labour in October 1974. In Benn's industrial strategy it recognised an existential threat to its power and privileges driven forward by an eloquent and effective socialist in a vital ministerial position who had support across the extra-parliamentary left and trade union movement.

It was not always obvious to Benn's many enemies that he had far less power and leverage within the government than they supposed. They perceived a phalanx of socialist ministers around Wilson whereas with the exception of Benn, Heffer and Hart the most left-wing, such as Michael Foot, were barely socialist at all in anything but rhetoric and vague historic sentimentality. The remains of the Bevanite "soft left" around Foot had a limited and paternalistic conception of transferring socio-economic power to the working class. Bevanite socialism was essentially the provision of beneficent social legislation such as the creation of bodies like the Health and Safety Executive (HSE) and the Advisory, Conciliation and Arbitration Service (ACAS), which through their tri-partite nature (i.e. they were usually run by commissioners appointed by the government, the CBI and the TUC) allowed the organised labour movement to influence certain aspects of the employment relationship in British industry.

Benn sought to be more transformative than that, but he was fatally hindered by two things. Firstly, although far ahead of his Cabinet colleagues in conceiving of Labour's socialist challenge as about extending democracy (economic as well as political) he had not really thought through its full implications, nor brought major left-wing trade union leaders like Jones and Scanlon with him. Secondly, he diverted his energies and political capital in to another great struggle, one that arguably he should have marginalised or postponed until he had secured real advances on the industrial front. But for Benn the campaign against membership of the EEC was part and parcel of his core political and economic philosophy and could not be sidelined. Hence he pushed for and secured the historic referendum on UK membership of the EEC. Having lost that, his subsequent removal killed any hope of an extension of industrial democracy within British industry and left radical trade unionists such as the Lucas Aerospace Combine with few friends at ministerial level.[10]

The outcomes of the battles over the Industry Act and the EEC Referendum "marked the end of a moderately radical period of Labour government in which the trade unions and the base of the Labour Party had the capacity to exert left pressure on a reluctant administration".[11] Wilson had skilfully used the Referendum campaign to remove his most troublesome socialist ministers – he fired Heffer for making an anti-EEC speech in the Commons, he moved Benn from Industry, and he offered Judith Hart a lesser post in Transport away from her area of expertise in International Relations and her commitment to solidarity with Third World liberation movements. She refused the demotion and resigned (to be replaced by Reg Prentice who after being deselected by his local party two years later promptly defected to the Conservatives). With a lamentable lack of insight or foresight the TUC gave little support to Benn, Heffer and Hart. The industrial strategy, with its demands that trade unions step up to assume national responsibilities and strategic leadership in industry, had always made the unions nervous. They were mostly content to see it diluted as long as the Social Contract gave them access to Labour ministers and influence over progressive employment legislation. It was left to Hart to draw the bigger picture in her resignation speech in which she said bluntly that if the government sought to solve the economic crisis by capitalist methods and to abandon its socialist policies it would "fail to solve the crisis and will betray the Labour movement".

Freed from ministerial restraint, she went further in an article for the *Guardian* in July. After summarising the powers and ability of multi-national companies to escape domestic govern-ments' economic control she stated that pricing policies and policies of expansion or contraction were now determined in an international context, and "As for hopes of regional job creation, and the ending of the social injustice which has blighted Scotland, Wales and the north for so many generations – forget them, unless we do what needs to be done".[12] This was an accurate prediction. For the rest of 1975 and throughout 1976 the government moved steadily towards the burial of whatever remained of its Keynesianism, let alone its socialism. As Benn had predicted, no sooner was he removed than Labour's enemies came back for more.

Chapter Twelve

The Moment of Defeat

In retrospect it is easy to see that the most significant development of this period was the election of Margaret Thatcher as Leader of the Conservative Party in February 1975. This was not so obvious at the time. In some respects a semi-comic figure to the British public (she was known as "Thatcher the milk snatcher" after her decision as Heath's Education Secretary to remove free school milk from poorer children) her hard right politics were not widely understood or even fully formed. But under the guidance of intellectual mentors like Keith Joseph and tough strategists from the fringes of the security services like Airey Neave and Brian Crozier she would develop into a formidable figure that the left continued to underestimate. In an analysis of Eric Hobsbawm's influential 1978 article "The Forward March of Labour Halted?", left-wing historian Tristram Hunt concludes "The tragedy is that, unable to cast off old orthodoxies (or, for that matter, factional grievances) it was not the men of the left that took heed of Marx's insight that men must make their own history, but a woman of the right".[1]

She did not make it alone. After the wave of social and industrial militancy that washed over Britain from 1968 until at least 1975 the right began to rally and find a voice. One vital part of that voice was the newly self-confident and aggressive yellow journalism of Rupert Murdoch's *The Sun*, which by the mid 1970s was beginning to rival, in sales terms, the still moralistic and Labourist *Daily Mirror* (it did not finally overtake the *Mirror* in sales until 1978). *The Sun* was no accident, nor was it unintelligent. In the opinion of the *Mirror*'s finest journalist *The Sun* had a "coherent world view" that promoted and popularised Thatcher's politics by "the sport of public vilification and the gleeful fly posting of misfortune".[2] It worshiped money, sex and power but drew its dissatisfied working class readership in with the promise that these things might be theirs if not for the "vested interests" of the trade unions and the threat to enrichment posed by a Marxist left led by Tony Benn. It left real vested interests – epitomised by Murdoch himself, who had inherited his wealth and been given his first Australian newspaper proprietorship as a present from his father – entirely alone. Although the *Mirror* was increasingly divided and demoralised by the popularity of *The Sun* it still gave space to world-class investigative journalism from the likes of John Pilger and, even in the bleak 1980s, Paul Foot. *The Sun* was the malignant dark twin of the *Mirror* metastasizing within British society. It was invaluable to Thatcher and her political project.

That project began to stir in the middle of the 1970s. Thatcher's election was the switch but the current spread out from covert "black ops" like Clockwork Orange and the work of the ISC to the extremes of intellectual and popular culture. At the core of the British state Treasury mandarins began to assess economic policy through the lens of Hayek and Friedman, although these free market gurus were clearly antipathetic to the Keynesian analysis and social democratic politics of the elected government. Of equal significance, the tide of radical popular culture seen in *Play for Today* and overtly political dramas like *Days of Hope* and *Bill Brand* (Trevor Griffith's 11 part prime time ITV drama about an ex- Trotskyist activist who becomes a left-wing Labour MP only to encounter compromise, defeat and disillusionment) began to stall and reverse. 1975 saw the debut of two iconic and extremely popular TV programmes that would go on to define 1970s British TV – *The Sweeney* and *Fawlty Towers*. Both were set in dysfunctional and failing worlds and had as heroes frustrated men who seethed with anger and impatience at the social and institutional constraints of the British social democratic welfare state. In their different ways DI Jack Regan and Basil

Fawlty were just waiting for Thatcherism to arrive.

In some respects it already had. The power of the financial markets to steer government economic policy did not arise solely from Thatcher's "Big Bang" deregulation of the City in 1986. Heath's abolition of Bank of England controls on bank lending in 1971 and the subsequent floating of the pound meant that credit and exchange rates were basically guided by interest rates alone. In June 1975 there was a severe "run on the pound". The stock market went into free fall, and in the absence of an interventionist price and import control policy the only way to appease the markets and avert increasing inflation was to contain the unions' pay claims. Healey began to apply ferocious pressure on the TUC to agree a variant on the Social Contract. Jack Jones had already raised the possibility of wage increases being awarded on a flat-rate basis, i.e. all employees in all professions would get literally the same amount of increase in the next pay round.[3] For those on higher wages the increase would be small. For those on the lowest it would be higher than usual. In return the government committed itself to policies to increase the wider "social wage" – rent controls, food subsidies, higher pensions. This became the basis for the preferred approach.

The biggest test for the policy was if it would get through the TGWU Annual Conference in Blackpool 30 June-4 July 1975. With a thousand delegates devoting an entire day solely to debating the proposal and the wider Social Contract, it was a demonstration of open, representative decision making that the bastions of establishment power in Britain – the City, Whitehall, the Security Services – would never have countenanced for themselves. After a vigorous debate the policy was supported by a large majority, an indication of the level of grass roots support within the unions for the basic approach of the Social Contract at the time. After haggling with Healey about the exact amount of the flat rate "cap" the TUC agreed that unions would restrict their pay claims to no more than £6 per a week. This was below inflation but also above what many lower paid workers would have achieved without it. Jones told the TGWU full time officials who had the job of applying the policy in specific pay bargaining rounds, "No one is claiming this is the ideal solution, but it is the best we can achieve at the present time. It is fair and socially just in its application".[4]

This was not entirely true. In the next twelve months inflation went down from 25% to 12%. Workers had undeniably contributed to battling inflation (though some professional occupations tried to breach the £6 cap, pleading special "differentials") but whilst unions moderated their wage claims, sterling continued to flow out of the country, aided by City institutions that had demanded there be no "siege economy". Having rejected the options offered by the AES the government wriggled and twisted to find solutions to capital flight and the weakening of British industry. In December 1975 Healey shifted slightly and accepted Kaldor's proposals for limited import quotas. He and Trade Secretary Peter Shore suggested a minimal quota of 0.16% of Britain's total imports. But it was too little, too late. Even with the quota, whose effects would take months to feed through, the government urgently needed a loan from the IMF to tide it over. In November it had already taken the first fateful step towards its own self-destruction as an independent entity implementing policies decided upon by Labour Party members and put successfully to the electorate in two General Elections. The IMF wanted security for its loans and according to its own criteria the security that was necessary was public spending cuts to the UK's health, education, and welfare budgets. These the Labour government began to set in motion after Healey bluntly told the Cabinet "Some of our creditors do not believe in incomes policies – they want cuts in public expenditure".[5]

The cuts in expenditure would be delivered at the worst possible time, as unemployment continued to escalate. In Autumn 1975 it officially passed the one and a half million mark.

Although trade unions were temporarily quiescent as they abided by their part of the Social Contract, others were not, questioning what use the Social Contract was if it did not protect working class people from unemployment. The Right to Work Campaign was launched by the IS and a variety of unaffiliated political and union activists. Although it was labelled an IS front it was a genuine reflection of anger about mass unemployment. This drove through to local and regional Right to Work initiatives that came together in a national Right to Work March from Manchester to London in March 1976. It started small but became a political and media story as it grew in size and approached London. The March had not been a dour trudge but a live solidarisitic demonstration with marchers visiting picket line and places of work on the way to propagandise and forge links. By the time it arrived at the climactic event at London's Royal Albert Hall it had 5,500 marchers and had been physically harassed by the police at Staples Corner as it entered London, leading to resistance and 44 arrests.[6] It did not alter government policy directly but it had great symbolic and emotional impact.

The pressures became too much for Harold Wilson. For reasons that to this day remain unclear, in March 1976 he unexpectedly resigned as Labour Leader and Prime Minister. The immediate cause may have been a vote in Parliament by thirty-seven left-wing Labour MPs against proposed cuts to public spending contained in the February Public Expenditure White Paper. The government was defeated, although it survived in office after Labour Whips manufactured a Vote of Confidence the next day in which the rebels felt obliged to support the government to stop it from collapsing.[7] After this Wilson may have seen the writing on the wall. Certainly he had no vision or optimism for the future, and his health was also failing. The extent to which MI5's continuing efforts to smear and undermine him (seen in the Clockwork Orange black propaganda material that seeped from Northern Ireland into London political gossip) finally drove him from office is still subject to conjecture. If it was the long standing agenda of elements within the security services to remove Wilson it was a very ill considered strategy, for when the Labour Party held its leadership election there arose the possibility that Foot, or even Benn, might be elected and therefore become Prime Minister. In the end Wilson's resignation made little difference to history. He was replaced by Jim Callaghan who, though personally more affable and less paranoid, shared all of Wilson's political positions.

Aside from the travails of the economy Callaghan inherited social and demographic tensions about which he and his ilk – aging white Labour leaders who came to politics in the 1930s – had little grasp or sympathy. By the mid-1970s British society was increasingly schizophrenic about race. Many of the young white working class, their social horizons expanded by the opening up of higher education, were shedding the prejudices of their parents. Black cultural influences like soul and reggae were going mainstream. Bob Marley had broken into Britain with "I Shot the Sherriff" (1973) and "No Woman, No Cry" (1975) and black British bands like The Real Thing and Hot Chocolate were wildly popular (in July 1976 The Real Thing's "You to Me Are Everything" topped the charts for three weeks). On the other hand Enoch Powell's anti-immigration "Rivers of Blood" speech in 1968 had revealed and legitimised widespread xenophobia amongst swathes of middle and working-class Britons. The reasons for this were complex and sometimes reflected cultural conservatism more than outright racism, but the effect was to propel a strain of native fascism into the political limelight. Even though there were only about 2 million black and Asian Britons amongst a total population of 56 million people, the hitherto small and marginal National Front began to make inroads in local elections.

In June 1976 in Southall, London, an Asian man, Gurdip Singh Chaggar, was stabbed to death by a gang of white youths. After local Asians demonstrated the police blanketed the area and began "stop and search" tactics on Asian youngsters. A local leader of the British National Party (BNP) publicly declared of Chaggar's murder "One down, One million to go" and was charged with incitement to racial hatred. The jury cleared him and the Judge sent him on his way with the comment "By all means propagate your views".[8] Amidst the heatwave of the summer of 1976, as temperatures topped 80 and then 90 degrees for weeks on end, racial tensions in London exploded at the Notting Hill Carnival. The police had increased their numbers at the Carnival to an unprecedented 1,600 officers. Confrontations between revellers and police escalated until the police moved in to make an arrest, which local youths resisted. Riots spread across the Carnival with 60 arrests and 456 people injured in the fighting. Significantly even the mainstream media began to question if the police's tactics were heavy handed and had sparked the events they all condemned.

It was not the only meltdown. Throughout June and July 1976 Sterling continued to fall and inflation began to rise again. UK government bonds usually sold to finance the Public Sector Borrowing Requirement (PSBR) were not being bought. Healey applied to the IMF for another line of credit but this time the IMF wanted substantial cuts in return. After several long and brutal Cabinet debates about accepting this the government committed to £1b in public expenditure cuts and a further £1b increase in employee's National Insurance contributions. Even this was not enough. Prompted by hard right Republicans in Washington (Healey said that the US Treasury Secretary, multi-millionaire bond trader Bill Simon, was "far to the right of Genghis Khan") the IMF made it clear that any further loan would require systemic reform of public expenditure.[9] Unbeknown to the government significant players in the City were already working closely with the US Treasury. Greenwells, the City's leading brokerage firm in long dated government stocks, was secretly sending its daily gilt-edged market reports to Bill Simon through a channel at the US Embassy. As both Simon and Greenwell's premier analyst Gordon Pepper shared a hard-right monetarist ideology (Pepper advised Thatcher on monetary issues in the 1980s) the reports were unlikely to have been politically neutral.[10] Simon in turn informed the IMF of Washington's priorities.

The TUC finally began to wake up to the scale of the threat. Up to this point it had been scrupulous in delivering its side of the bargain on industrial militancy and wage restraint. Driven by deep and in some cases unquestioning loyalty to the Labour government (which after the battles with the Tories and Michael Foot's provision of what he rightly called "the most powerful pro-trade union legislation ever put on the statute book", was perhaps understandable) the TUC and its senior figures such as Jones and Scanlon had demonstrated the sense of responsibility and concern for the national economy that the media so often accused them of lacking, and which their detractors in the trading rooms and clearing banks of the City so conspicuously did lack. It is a myth that TUC "barons" forced a militant membership chafing at the bit for strike action to swallow the Social Contract. At least until 1976 the falling off of strike action after Labour took office was an obvious grace period to see what a trade union supported government could do, and partially at least approval of what it had done. But by the end of 1976 individual unions were restless. Alan Fisher, General Secretary of the militant public sector workers union NUPE, told a special TUC conference that had just endorsed "Phase II" of further wage restraint (increases limited to no more than £2.50 to £4 per week) that they should not become "mesmerised by the process itself rather than considering the results that it achieves". He pointed out that whilst labour was showing national responsibility, capital was not, and that it was "dangerous for the movement to accept incorporation into the apparatus of the State" which was not and never would be a neutral body.[11]

The TUC was increasingly alert to such criticism and looking for more out of the Social Contract. Its report on Phase II concluded that if it was to be fair and effective it must be accompanied by major reforms of the banking and financial system. It demanded a full governmental inquiry into short-term capital flight so as to "assess the reasons for the speculation and identity of those actively engaged in speculation". Trade union leaders like Clive Jenkins were now vociferous in demanding import and capital controls and a coherent response to the economic crisis that applied the AES. Inside the Treasury Kaldor bombarded Healey with suggestions for dealing with the economic crisis that he hoped would avoid the necessity for a huge IMF loan, the conditions of which would forbid the import controls he considered so important. He proposed a £1 billion cut in public spending, a 5% payroll tax, a car tax surcharge, extending the limited capital export controls Healey had already introduced and an "import deposit scheme" that required those importing manufactures to deposit 200% of their value in the Bank of England for a year.[12] When the Treasury supported the spending cut but ignored all the other proposals Kaldor resigned.

It is not clear to what extent Callaghan was informed of the existence of viable economic options to avoid a large IMF loan and the conditions that would accompany it. He was not an economist and he was heavily influenced by his son-in-law Peter Jay (at the time the Economics Editor of the *Times*, later appointed UK Ambassador to Washington), who was a leading advocate for the new monetarism. As such Callaghan would have no truck with the full AES or even the TUC's watered down version of it. But unlike Healey he did at least inform the party he led that he had now officially abandoned the Keynesian social democracy on which he had built his career and which they had hoped Labour would deliver in government. In September 1976 he took the case for monetarism to the Labour Party conference. There he delivered a speech written for him by Jay that buried for good Labour's 1973 Programme and its 1974 General Election Manifestos. "We used to think you could spend your way out of recession, and increase employment by cutting taxes and increasing government spending. I tell you in all candour" he told stunned delegates, "that option no longer exists, and in so far as it ever did exist, it worked on each occasion since the war to inject bigger doses of inflation into the economy, followed by higher levels of unemployment as the next step. Now ..." he concluded "... we must get back to fundamentals".[13] For Callaghan and Jay those fundamentals were simple – the analysis, priorities and necessities of the Market. They could not conceive of any alternative, although a more intellectual social democrat like Tony Crosland considered Callaghan's speech would breed "illiterate and reactionary views of public expenditure" and was a political gift to Margaret Thatcher.

Benn fought back. At the same conference he made the case for the NEC's separate economic policy document based on the AES, and delivered a rousing speech that started with the self-criticism that Labour had not advanced a coherent alternative to the doctrines of the Treasury and Bank of England. "The political vacuum we have left" he said "has been filled by many different voices. By the monetarists, by the nationalists, by the racialists, and by all who seek to divide working people from each other and to breed despair, so that we may be driven to lose faith in ourselves and our capacity to control our own destiny".[14] Policy makers in America were also concerned that Benn might yet swing the Labour Party around to an independent economic policy. William Rogers of the US State Department later admitted that the Republican administration and its placemen in the IMF were "concerned about Tony Benn precipitating a policy decision by Britain to turn its back on the IMF. If that had happened the whole system would have started to come apart".[15]

They need not have worried. The Labour government had no intention of spurning the IMF. In the same month Healey applied to the IMF for a £4b loan. The conditions laid down before it could be agreed were, as expected, exceptionally harsh including unprecedented cuts to public spending, especially the welfare bill, of £1bn in 1977-78 and a further £1.5bn in 1978-79. The conditions revealed the deep and fundamental differences at the heart of the Labour Party and the Labour government, differences that had been concealed or evaded before but that now, in the unforgiving light of the IMF's demands, tore the Cabinet apart. In a Memorandum from the Chancellor of 22nd November on "IMF Negotiations" Healey laid out the situation as he perceived it with stark clarity: "It is clear from the latest short-term forecasts that at the present planned levels of expenditure and taxation we shall face very severe financing problems over the next year or two, both at home and abroad".[16] He reported that the forecast for the PSBR for 1977-78 was nearly £11billion and the forecast deficit for the balance of payments the next year was nearly £3billion. Summarising the IMF discussions he had been conducting he reported that while the IMF "did not see it as its function to dictate policies to the UK Government", it had in fact done exactly that as it had "indicated a number of objectives which they believe we should need to adopt in order to persuade the Board and our main creditors that our policies are viable". Making clear what the agenda and priorities of the Fund actually were Healey reported that "the Fund team originally argued that, to have maximum effect, this adjustment should be achieved solely through savings on public expenditure". Faced with this Healey recommended that the government would have to make savings of £1 ½ billion in 1977-78, rising to a further £2billion in 1978-79.[17]

Although Benn did not, like Healey, have the formidable economic modelling resources of the Treasury at his disposal, he responded as best he could on 29th November in a Memorandum to the Cabinet entitled "The Real Choices Facing the Cabinet". Replying directly to Healey's 22nd November paper and the recommendations therein Benn concluded that "They would involve cuts into public services so deep as to endanger their basic function and cuts in social benefits that would put at risk the Social Contract".[18] With an internal self-criticism entirely absent from Healey's paper Benn said of the Alternative Strategy he recommended that "It is based on a plain recognition that the strategy we have followed since March 1974 has failed". He asserted that "The alternative strategy is based on the belief that the price we must pay for borrowing to finance a free trade policy is too high because it involves unacceptable levels of unemployment, unacceptably low levels of investment and progressive deterioration of our manufacturing capacity", concluding that "But if we are not seen to be defending our interests we cannot aspire to the national leadership which two General Elections have placed in our hands for the benefit of all".[19] The two memoranda could hardly have been more different. Whilst Benn placed these crucial decisions within a political context and sought to draw the consequences for the Labour Party, the trade unions and the working class they were ostensibly there to represent, Healey simply drove forward in a Treasury created vacuum.

Callaghan had other considerations. Just before the fateful decision on the IMF loan was about to be made the Cabinet Secretary Sir John Hunt informed him what the Permanent Secretary of the Ministry of Defence, Sir Frank Cooper, considered would be the effect on Britain's military spending of the cuts required by the IMF (the views of Labour's Secretary of State for Defence do not seem to have been discussed). Cooper considered that if, as a result of the IMF package, the MoD had to implement £100million of defence cuts "the view would probably be taken" that the UK should scrap Polaris, the UK's independent nuclear missile force, rather than the more unwelcome option of cutting the British Army of the Rhine (British troops stationed in Germany to ostensibly deter Soviet invasion, in reality to enhance

Britain's status within NATO). Callaghan seems to have worried more about this than the effect on social spending. In a tense phone conversation with President Gerald Ford he used the possibility of the UK withdrawing from its military commitments to pressurise Washington to lean on the IMF and avoid certain loan conditions.[20]

Although the climactic, long and bitter Cabinet meetings of 1st and 2nd December 1976 that discussed the IMF loan and the conditions upon it were full of political and personal drama – the efforts of Benn, Foot and Shore to avert the loan and the cuts and to promote a practical alternative, Crosland's rejection of monetarist logic as "crazy" and "destructive of what he believed in his entire life" followed by his total collapse of morale and vote to support the cuts, Healey's sledgehammer insistence that the government had little choice but to swallow the IMF's conditions – there was never any real doubt that a Labour administration that had already reversed its commitment to a socialist economic policy and conceded so much to the emerging new financial orthodoxy espoused by the Treasury and the IMF would baulk at this last surrender. When Callaghan, who had affected a sober and reflective neutrality during the marathon debate, finally weighed in behind Healey the majority of the Cabinet dutifully followed him.

There was still a fear that Labour MPs would not support cuts on such a scale. When it became clear that Callaghan and Healey had the Cabinet majority they needed to agree the IMF conditions, Callaghan warned his colleagues that he had been told by Sir John Hunt and Labour's Chief Whip that on no account was the package of measures to be put before the wider Parliamentary party. In a revealing insight in to where real power lay in society, the unelected Cabinet Secretary Hunt told the Prime Minister that he could not risk Labour MPs having a say in the decision for if they were not supportive "sterling could fall through the floor in literally minutes".[21] The Virtual Senate would decide. Faced with this Callaghan told the Cabinet that there was "an absolute need to avoid any legislation arising from this package" because "we could not rely on the Parliamentary party to carry it through".[22] It was an unnecessary concern. Hunt and the Chief Whip had overestimated the independence of Labour MPs and in the event most of them accepted Healey's logic. If there was a "consensus" position it was around neither Healey nor Benn but Crosland – i.e a pained and reluctant acceptance of the cuts as inevitable. "It is the moment of defeat, and we have to recognise it" Benn confided to his diary.[23]

The humiliating nature of the defeat was underlined by the "Letter of Intent" that the IMF extorted out of the government as part of the final package. The Letter was stark. Amongst other commitments the government had to state that "The Government remains firmly opposed to generalised restrictions on trade, and does not intend to introduce restrictions for balance of payments purposes". Reflecting the policy priorities of the financial markets and City traders, the Letter also made the government pledge that it would not "impose new or intensify existing restrictions on payments and transfers of current international transactions".[24] The enforcers had done their work. The victim duly signed.

A rubicon had been crossed, and for no good reason. It was later admitted that the Treasury data that Healey had relied upon and that emphasised the seriousness of the "crisis" – that the PSBR was unsustainably high with the effect on the deficit that would follow – had been inaccurate, either by design or incompetence or a mixture of the two. Although the Treasury's reports to Healey had been that the PSBR for 1976-77 would be £10.5bn it actually turned out to be £2bn less than that, and thus the difference exceeded the level of public spending cuts that the IMF considered essential.[25] In his memoirs Healey later accused the Treasury of "deliberately misleading the government" and voiced his suspicion that "Treasury officials deliberately overstated public spending in order to put pressure on govern-ments which were reluctant to cut it".[26] He never apologised to Benn, though.

In a wider sense it was not about the PSBR or the deficit. The IMF's operation was political. It was designed to erase what remained of the socialist aspirations in Labour's 1973 Programme and 1974 Manifestos, to contain Tony Benn, and to reassure the City that the nostrums and priorities of the financial sector, not elected politicians, were now setting the economic agenda. Where more conventional though more lauded intellects like Crosland and Healey had been wrong footed at every turn, Benn had seen it coming. In the first days of the new Labour government, when he was still fighting for industrial policies that might have given the government more control over its destiny, he had a premonition of how that struggle would go and what it would mean for the Keynesian welfarism that had taken Britain through the years since 1945 – "My own belief is that this consensus is in fact coming to an end, and that although we shall have a short honeymoon, we are going to either see it crack under inflationary pressure in which wage demands will play a part, be driven back to statutory wage control which is quite unacceptable, or to some other form of control of the trade unions. To this extent I do believe that society is actually in the process of break up".[27]

At the time Benn could hardly predict that the Labour government would be followed by a right-wing Conservative Prime Minister who not only agreed with him but also believed that this was a good thing, that there was in fact "no such thing as society" and to the extent that there was, it deserved to break up. The alternative to a deregulated, privatised economy and society had been fractured in the 1970s. Both variants of that alternative – traditional social democratic welfarism, and a more creative socialist alternative based on the AES, planning agree-ments to guarantee strategic investment, and economic democracy – had been shut down, brutally terminated by the emerging "Washington Consensus" expounded by the IMF and free-market ideologues like Friedman and Thatcher.

For a brief period in the 1970s there was another option. If progressed with vigour and commitment it might have avoided the damage subsequently inflicted on the UK economy by the City and the financial sector, the crippling of its domestic industry, ever escalating social inequalities and the creation of a parasitic super-rich elite within the virtual tax haven of central London. That option is now almost forgotten, and is either passed over or misrepresented in what has become the "official version" of the crucial period 1974-76. That option no longer exists.

Conclusion

Passion in action

Like the German Weimar Republic of the late 1920s and early 1930s, Britain in the 1970s was a period of great iconoclasm and stress, bursting with cultural, social and sexual liberation. Working Class people asserted their rights and crossed boundaries. Marxist and Socialist movements campaigned and debated vigorously, often at cross-purposes. Left-wing politicians struggled with immense political and economic problems. And waiting in the wings were right-wing authoritarians with few scruples about tactics and allies.[1] From this perspective the turning point of post war British history is to be found in the neglected period 1974-76, in the undermining and rejection of the radical economic and industrial policies contained in Labour's 1973 Programme and 1974 General Election Manifestos, and the change of direction forced on the government (against minimal resistance by the Prime Minister and Chancellor) in 1976. The new direction was formally signed and sealed in 1979 with the election of Margaret Thatcher.

After the IMF crisis of 1976 any notion of a progressive Social Contract was mortally wounded. The Social Contract and its chief advocates had delivered substantial and positive reforms in 1974-76, not least historic advances for the position of women in British society such as child benefit, sex discrimination legislation and the first application of the Equal Pay Act. To a certain extent the raising of the state pension by up to a quarter, price and rent controls, health and safety legislation and better employment protections went some way to balance wage restraint, which in its first two years was a genuine trade off with government.[2] But the discipline and solidarity of the trade unions in abiding by it despite the rate of inflation was never understood or appreciated by Denis Healey and the Treasury (Jack Jones said he could never tell them apart). Hence Phases III and IV of wage restraint were not the same beast as Phases I and II. Phase III allowed a maximum increase of 10% but in a context of falling real wages and rising unemployment the TUC did not formally accept it, a sign of things to come. Although Phase III held and by 1978 inflation fell to 10% the government, with Jones now retired and his successors angry and disillusioned with the Social Contract, unwisely choose to go to Phase IV, which limited pay increases to 5%. This was as fatal a step as the quiet assassination of the industrial strategy, Callaghan's rejection of Keynesianism and the acceptance of the IMF's Letter of Intent.

1976 was not the end of political struggle. There were events of real political significance in 1977-79, most especially the upsurge of organised anti-racist street protest and of course the "Winter of Discontent". Although the wave of public sector strike action between November 1978 and March 1979 was on a scale unseen since the 1920s (on January 22nd 1979 one and half million public sector workers stopped work on a national day of action, with a plethora of official and unofficial strikes across public services during the winter) it could hardly be said to be without cause. Public sector wage increases had been pegged below inflation for several years and were hitting workers at the same time as IMF mandated cuts were feeding through and beginning to slash jobs and services. With inflation at 10% the unions' agreement to the 5% limit would have meant a serious cut in living standards for their members without even the quid pro quo of a Labour government delivering on other objectives such as safeguarding investment in public services. In addition, and to add to the dramatic imagery of the strikes, unlike the mild winter of 1973/74 at the time of the Three Day Week the winter of 1978/79 was exceptionally harsh, with heavy snow and arctic conditions adding to the paralysis experienced in urban centres.

Tellingly, it was the provision of services by striking workers rather than their denial that most exercised right-wing commentary. Hence the hysterical reaction to the situation in Hull, where as part of a road hauliers strike a TGWU "Dispensation Committee" effectively controlled delivery and distribution of food and fuel supplies into the city. Because of Hull's unique geographical situation, isolated on the east coast with at the time only one main road into the city, the strikers had a strong position. Of particular terror to the employers and the media that supported them were the daily meetings of the Dispensation Committee to which local employers, farmers, and managers had to attend with formal requests for delivery of goods.[3] The Committee was scrupulous in allowing food and fuel through to hospitals and schools but all other distribution was on its own terms and as it thought fit, consistent with the strike. In London the Transport Secretary Bill Rodgers (who in 1975 had enjoyed breakfasts at the Dorchester with his Tory allies in the pro-EEC campaign, and in 1981 would be one of the "Gang of Four" who left Labour to form the Social Democratic Party, cutting a huge slice from Labour's vote and effectively handing the 1983 General Election to Thatcher) was talking to the Cabinet Office's Civil Contingencies Unit about sending the Army in to Hull to remove the Committee. Instead the CCU co-ordinated with TGWU full time officials to agree criteria for deliveries, which were then passed to the Committee who carried on much as before.

Actions like this worried the political elite more than a few strikers causing disruption to rubbish collection or funerals (which were gleefully welcomed by the media as weapons with which to demonise all strikers and trade unions, no matter the dispute or the justice of their case). It was *lack of disruption*, of demonstrable willingness and ability by working class people to carry on the running of services and government without management and civil service control, that was the threat most feared. In that sense the brief rise of Dispensation Committees in

Hull and elsewhere were one of the few political developments in the 1970s that actually merited the right's hyperbolic language about "revolution". The Dispensation Committees were a mild variant of the Soviets (Workers Councils) that arose in the 1905 and 1917 Russian Revolutions and whilst the mainly non-ideological British trade union movement may not have recognised them as such, the British ruling class certainly did.

Most commentary considers the Winter of Discontent in isolation, with a few references to rampaging inflation (although by 1978 it was falling) and public sector unions' non-contextualised "pay demands". Yet the causal linkage between the government's acceptance of the IMF loan conditions laid out in the 1976 Letter of Intent – in effect, to make nearly £4 billion pounds worth of cuts in public spending by 1979 – and the inevitable push back in 1978/79 could hardly be clearer. The IMF had not prescribed its requirements in a political vacuum and a minority of more objective historians have disinterred its underlying agenda. Kathleen Burk, in an acute dissection of the real relations of power between the UK and the US at the time discusses the crisis of 1976 from the perspective of an IMF that received the bulk of its funding, personnel and resources from the US. As such it was therefore concerned that the Labour government was "engaged in activities which very much worried the US Government" – specifically that if the Labour left had its way it might institute a "siege economy" and withdraw from NATO. In response "The US Treasury in particular, but also the US State Department and the National Security Council, working through the IMF, required fundamental changes in British economic policy, in terms of cuts in public expenditure, unemployment policy, credit policy and interest rates".[4] It achieved its short term objective with control of UK government spending and its longer term objective through the election of Margaret Thatcher. Economic neo-liberalism, with some minor deviations on the fringes of social policy, has been in the ascendant in the UK ever since.

Nor was the UK a lone victim. At virtually the same time the IMF had aborted Jamaica's experiment in democratic socialism. Although Michael Manley and the PNP were re-elected in a landslide in 1976 the Jamaican economy was under strain due to American destabilisation and an orchestrated capital flight. The IMF attempted to make the same sort of deal with the Jamaican government that it had with the British – a loan on the condition that the government severely restrict social spending and abandon nationalisation, especially of the crucial US owned Bauxite companies. Manley's first instinct was to resist, and he refused the terms. The gloves came off and a CIA directed campaign of economic sabotage, assisted by a virulently anti-Manley Jamaican media, began to poison Jamaican politics. Gunfights broke out between rival political parties. Manley sought to raise finance from political allies like Cuba but the required funds were not available. In the end he had to accept the IMF's "Standby Agreement" of 1977 whereby in return for £38 million to ease the balance of payments crisis the PNP had to institute massive cuts to public spending. The repudiation of the policies on which it had achieved victory in 1976 led to disillusionment with the PNP, the ascendance of the right-wing opposition led by Edward Seaga and its election in 1980 on a monetarist economic programme. As Manley put it after his defeat, "What we did was challenge the power of the western economic structure. This was one country that tried to challenge hegemony and was not successful".[5]

British trade unions in 1978/79, whether they perceived it or not, were also challenging hegemony. As were other movements that demonstrated an ability to resist what by the end of the decade was a shift to the right in the body politic. Standing four square against that shift – and, significantly, a grass roots led and determinedly street level initiative – was Rock Against Racism (RAR) and the Anti-Nazi League (ANL), the most effective and politically conscious reaction to the rise and electoral gains of the fascist National Front (NF). The NF was formed in 1967 but only started to take off in 1976 as the political consensus of the post war years truly fractured. In 1977 it received 19% of the vote in Hackney South and Bethnal Green and its ugly initials appeared scrawled on walls in inner city estates. It began to recruit alienated working class youth, helped unwittingly by the ambiguity of some of Punk's leading icons towards the symbols of fascism and nationalism. The Jam's first album cover was a Union Jack, The Sex Pistols wore swastika badges to shock bourgeois opinion and Johnny Rotten's "I hate hippies and what they stand for. I hate long hair ..." could have come from an NF thug.

But it was mainstream rock that led, indirectly, to the creation of RAR. In August 1976 Eric Clapton used one of his concerts to declare his vocal support for Enoch Powell. Challenges to Clapton were immediately published in *New Musical Express*, *Melody Maker* and *Socialist Worker*, and RAR was formed. Drawing its protest tactics from "French Surrealism, Marxist politics and the best of Punk"[6] RAR influenced The Clash, Sham 69 and Siouxsie and the Banshees to look critically at their fashion and design statements and to produce politically conscious, explicitly anti-racist protest songs. From this grew Two Tone music and overtly multiracial bands like The Specials and The Beat, later to produce the classic anti-Thatcher song "Stand Down, Margaret".

RAR had such impact because it threw back at the NF their own street level campaigning, most notoriously on 13 August 1977 in Lewisham, London, when a contingent of RAR and other left activists refused to disperse under police orders and broke the back of a large NF march. This led in its turn to the creation of the Anti-Nazi League, set up by London SWP organiser Paul Holborow, with Deputy General Secretary of the Engineers Union Ernie Roberts and Communications Officer of the Postal

Workers Union Peter Hain (both of whom would go on to become Labour MPs). The ANL brought together trade unions, left parties, writers, musicians, and actors. Although the bulk of the organisational heavy lifting was done by the SWP the ANL was a classic popular front with wide support. Its largest and most significant protests were a series of massive anti-racist carnivals, beginning in April 1978 in East London's Victoria Park where 80,000 people soaked up the ANL message while RAR put on The Clash, Tom Robinson, Stiff Little Fingers and X Ray Spex.[7] Shortly after this a smaller RAR festival was thrown in Brockwell Park in South London (as the marchers came down Railton Road they passed under a banner hung up by the South London Gay Community Centre proclaiming "Brixton Gays Welcome Anti-Fascists!"). More ANL carnivals followed in Manchester (35,000), Cardiff (5,000), Southampton (5,000) and Edinburgh (8,000) and local ANL groups sprung up across the country. By the time of the violent clash with the NF at Southhall in London in April 1979 in which the Special Patrol Group clubbed teacher Blair Peach to death, the ANL's wall of resistance to the NF had done the latter significant damage. In the 1979 General Election its vote fell to 1.3% of the total.

The ANL had risen to the challenge of the NF and the potential growth of a mass racist movement by not retreating to comfortable redoubts and not looking to politicians for salvation, and above all by creating a confident radical message for its primarily working class target base to support and enjoy. In similar fashion the British feminist movement had diversified since its re-emergence in the 1960s out of the lifestyle concerns of wealthy American feminists like Betty Friedan to an engagement with community and working class politics. In the fervid political atmosphere of the 1970s the British women's movement began to fracture between those who moved away from the mainstream to forge a separatist radical feminist agenda and those who wished to engage with the left and trade unions to advance the needs of working class women and make feminism as directly relevant to those women as possible.

Beyond the Fragments exemplified this strand of thinking. Co-authored by the socialist feminists Sheila Rowbotham, Hilary Wainwright and Lynne Segal, it was published as a long pamphlet in 1979 and was an immediate sensation on the left. It was then expanded and republished as a book in 1980 to coincide with a large and influential conference in Leeds on the issues it raised. Rowbotham had argued in her seminal book *Women, Resistance and Revolution* (1972) that whilst the roots of women's subservience lay in capitalism and class hierarchy, socialist resistance to these often disregarded the rights of women once in office or power. She cited the Russian, Chinese and Cuban revolutions as examples where there was inevitably a reassertion of traditional gender roles as male revolutionaries dominated the new power structures and relied on women's unpaid domestic labour as much as the men they had replaced. But *Beyond the Fragments* went further than this and claimed that the basis of the traditional revolutionary project – Leninism in theory and practice – was simply not suited to achieving liberatory social objectives, being inherently dogmatic and authoritarian. Wainwright, in her part of the book, focused instead on alternative centres of resistance to capitalism and the profit motive. She analysed the 1970s as a period in which "industrial militants, plus the new movements of students, women, and black organisations, were quickly thrown on to their own resources. In this situation, the women's movement, solidarity movements with international struggles, many shop stewards and local action committees, the anti-fascist movement, theatre groups, alternative newspapers, militant tenants, squatters and community groups have themselves become a political focus".[8]

This kind of criticism and approach was derided by Leninists like the SWP. Demonstrating a blithe disregard for women, sexual politics and the home, it dismissed the book as "not being read on the steel picket lines nor passed around among militants at Longbridge".[9] Be that as it may, *Beyond the Fragments* struck a chord with women on the left who wished to advance a concrete and realistic feminist agenda but found the style, practices and assumptions of left parties and trade unions profoundly alienating and insensitive. Lynne Segal pointed out that women had a perspective on the welfare state that should be valued as "they came into contact with it more directly than men, in the form of welfare, nursery provision, and education and health services". It was this challenge not only to capitalist ideology and the newly elected Margaret Thatcher but also to the stolid and unconscious sexism of the traditional male left that made *Beyond the Fragments* so disruptive. The book conceded that winning a parliamentary majority was important but stressed this had to be on the basis of a strong extra-parliamentary alliance, which should be libertarian, inclusive and responsive to new social movements within Britain in the 1970s and 1980s. Significantly both Rowbotham and Wainwright went on to leading roles within Ken Livingstone's Greater London Council from 1980 to 1986, the most ambitious and at least partially successful effort by the British left since 1951 to transform society in a progressive direction.

Perhaps the greatest missed opportunity was on industrial democracy. The Labour government was never keen on party policy as set by the 1973 Conference and it was not until August 1975 that it moved to create a committee of enquiry headed by Sir Alan Bullock, the historian and biographer of Ernest Bevin, to look into feasible schemes for instituting industrial democracy. The committee consisted of three union leaders (Jack Jones, David Lea and Clive Jenkins), three company chairmen and some legal and academic experts. It published its report in January 1977 with a minority dissent from the employers' representatives. Jones and Jenkins did a solid job of ensuring that the TUC's preferred approach – adoption of the EEC's 5th Directive on Company Law, based on German co-determination policy by which German union federations had a real say in the direction of German industries – had made it into the majority report. If adopted this would mean that companies employing over 2,000 workers would have equal representation on their Boards of employer and employee representatives.[10]

The potential increase in union leverage and influence was enormous. Unfortunately British trade union conservatism kicked in, with the two extremes of the union movement (the left-wing NUM and the right-wing EEPTU) united in their deep suspicion of anything which either limited complete freedom of adversarial collective bargaining or raised the prospect of genuine industrial democracy. The CBI campaigned vehemently against Bullock's proposals, which might have given those unions who opposed it pause to wonder why. Faced with opposition from both sides the government quietly dropped the idea. The proposals, whilst delivering a top down, bureaucratic version of industrial democracy, had opened the door to a level of strategic influence in British industry that the unions would never come close to again. It was not the kind of workers control the IWC advocated but it had the potential to develop upwards to provide input on the government's own strategic investment decisions and downwards to the engagement of the shop floor in the same manner as the Lucas Aerospace Combine (itself regarded with suspicion by some union officials). That potential was lost.

The LA Combine's creative and startlingly original ideas for an Alternative Corporate Plan fell victim to the change of political direction within the Labour government after the removal of Tony Benn from Industry. After this there was no longer a sympathetic reception within Whitehall for ideas from the shop floor about a transition to socially useful production. With Planning Agreements merely voluntary and of limited scope, and the NEB denied any role but propping up failing companies, there was in any case no economic architecture to support and develop such ideas. Hence when the Combine put its full plan to LA senior managers at a meeting in January 1976 the response was cold. Management merely said it would take it away and consider it and reply at a second meeting in April. That meeting was cancelled and the Company's reply was sent in the post. Summarising with barely concealed hostility the Plan's proposals for diversifying into "socially acceptable/useful products", the Company responded that "It cannot accept that aircraft, military and civil, do not have a social utility", and stiffly concluded "The company reminds the report's authors that it has a long standing capability and reputation for producing a wide range of aerospace system and components, and believes that the only way to secure jobs in the market economy is to manufacture the products which the company is best at producing efficiently and profitably".[11] In reality the company's response had little, if anything, to do with the actual ideas in the Plan. It was the Plan's very existence and premise – that workers on their own could devise a viable strategy for diversified, original and socially useful production, implicitly calling into question the need for both management and, ultimately, owners – that affronted them.

The immense potential of the Combine's Alternative Plan would never be realised although it would later become influential as a precursor to the "Green New Deal" that environmental campaigners and trade unions developed in the 2000s. The failure to fully engage with the Alternative Plan, the Bullock Report or the ideas of the IWC did, however, reveal a huge intellectual vacuum within the British trade union movement. On the whole the British labour movement preferred to put its faith in two contrasting but equally unimaginative strategies – that a Labour government would pass employment legislation favourable to them and so cushion their existence and guarantee their future, or that a massive physical confrontation with the powers of the State would, without any remotely coherent plans for doing so, somehow overthrow a capitalist economic system and usher in a better one. One strategy hadn't worked. The other never could.

Unlike the left, the right had a cohesive and ruthless strategic plan and the will to carry it out. In 1977 one of Thatcher's key allies, the right-wing MP Nicholas Ridley wrote a paper for the Conservative Party Research Department that has come to be known as the Ridley Plan. In a memorandum of 8th July 1977 entitled "Final Report of the Nationalised Industries Policy Group" Ridley set out a detailed strategy for denationalising the UK's publicly owned industries and utilities. The thrust of the policy was not itself a secret although the scope of it was not admitted whilst the Tories were in opposition. But the meat was in the Confidential Annex "Countering the Political Threat". In the Annex Ridley told Thatcher that at some point their enemies would attempt to destroy the policy. They would find a reason for discontent and then "... the full force of the communist disruptors will be used to exploit that discontent". Predicting that "The most likely area is coal ..." Ridley made several recommendations, amongst which were to provoke a strike at time of the government's choosing, to stockpile coal in advance, to use the law to cut off money to strikers and their families, and to institute a "large, mobile squad of police" to physically crush the strike. Ridley concluded that these tactics should be enough "until the long term strategy of fragmentation can begin to work".[12]

Thatcher and Ridley carried out the plan. From 1979 the UK was plunged into a thirty-year experiment with neo-liberalism, deregulation and privatisation that fundamentally damaged British society. While mass unemployment, beyond anything the 1974-79 Labour government had struggled with, disfigured large parts of the social landscape and crippled trade unions' bargaining and leverage power, the harsh Victorian values of Thatcher's new Tories taught working class youth to look down and mind their place. Where once the BBC produced *The Rank and File* and *Days of Hope*, in the 1980s its finest dramas were *Boys from the Blackstuff* and *Edge of Darkness* in which those who dared resist the new privatised state were crushed and thrown away. Optimistic Glam Rock became angry Punk and despairing Ska. In 1972 Marc Bolan had sung "You won't fool the Children of the Revolution". In 1981 the Specials sang "This town is coming like a Ghost Town". The last epic British war film, *A Bridge Too Far* (1977), had lamented brave paratroopers defeated not by the enemy but by incompetent planning, imperial arrogance, bad luck and the weather. Thereafter British film entered a period of creative torpor redeemed only by occasional gems like *The Long Good Friday* (1980) with its razor-sharp satire on brute Thatcherism. Thatcher herself may have been removed from office in 1990 but the glorification of amoral ambition and enrichment pulsated throughout British culture in the 1980s and 1990s, exemplified in Peter Mandelson's admission that New Labour was "intensely relaxed about people getting filthy rich".

Yet in 2010, at the moment when the lessons from the neo-liberal experiment seemed about to be learnt, the Conservative-Liberal Democrat coalition government, with no electoral mandate to do so, regressed to the worst "Shock Doctrine" policies of Thatcher, Reagan and Pinochet. Since then trade unions have been attacked. Public sector pensions have been cut whilst the retirement age has been raised. Vital employment protections have been removed. Welfare claimants are attacked and demonised. Unprecedented spending cuts have decimated public services and local government. The UK reversed back into a double and triple dip recession and food banks appeared in every major city. In 2014 the UK seems, at best, to be experiencing a cyclical and not a structural recovery. Temporary recovery or not, core parts of the social fabric, untouched even by Thatcher, are now being sold off and privatised. These policies threaten to remove what is left of the British welfare state.[13]

What should be the left's response? Labour's call for "responsible capitalism" or the hope that a new party to the left of Labour and based on the trade unions will emerge and thrive in a very short time? Neither seems up to the challenges of the 21st century. Yet a challenge of equal (indeed, much greater) severity has been faced by the Greek left and they have responded with a creativity and maturity that puts the British left to shame. After the collapse of the Greek economy because of the failure of a debt loaded speculative financial system run by corrupt Greek plutocrats, the prime consideration for international bodies such as the European Central Bank and the IMF was to ensure that international investors (primarily German and American banks) were guaranteed full payback of their loans to the improvident Greek state. The "bail out" of Greece was not to rescue the country, still less the people, but to keep the wheels greased for the international financial system of which the rescuers were partners and beneficiaries. Thus in return for the bail out the "Troika" (the IMF, the ECB and the European Commission) imposed Memorandum II on the Greek government, requiring a 22% cut in the Greek Minimum Wage, a 15% cut in the state pension, 150,000 public sector job losses, and a massive wave of privatisation of state owned assets and utilities. The results were a replication of the effect of similar slash-and-burn policies under Pinochet in Chile. Unemployment and poverty skyrocketed and many segments of the Greek society were reduced to a barter economy as social services collapsed. But unlike Chile where there could be no protest the Troika made the mistake of imposing economic punishment on a country that was an EU state with democratic freedoms. In May 2011 massive protest erupted with the occupation of Syntagma Square in Athens. 50,000 protestors surrounded Parliament and there began what were to be seven General Strikes to protest austerity. "Committees of struggle" set up in many workplaces to resist the Troika's imposition of austerity.[14]

As PASOK, the Greek Socialist Party, was complicit in acceptance of Memorandum II and the resultant austerity programme, this resistance may have gone nowhere if not for the fact that the different strands of the non-PASOK Greek left were now working together under the broad banner of Syriza (the Greek initials of the Coalition of the Radical Left, Unitary Social Front). Syriza had emerged in 2004 as a result of a process dubbed the "Space for Dialogue for the Unity and Common Action of the Left" that had been proceeding for some years. The "Space" enabled various organizations and parties on the Greek left to park relatively unimportant ideological differences and to meet, discuss and agree common political actions against cuts to state pensions and welfare services. From here Syriza emerged as a genuinely inclusive, non-dogmatic alliance of the left that stands in firm opposition to austerity and to the terms of Memorandum II. Whilst PASOK has disintegrated Syriza is now the biggest party outside the discredited pro-austerity coalition government whereas in Britain, faced with the Labour Party's acceptance of "austerity-lite" the reaction of the disparate strands of the non-Labour left has been to carry on as usual. In 2014 the fact remains that unless and until groups such as the Coalition of Resistance, Left Unity, the SWP, the Socialist Party, the Socialist Labour Party, and the Trade Union and Socialist Coalition (TUSC) create their own "space for dialogue" and, crucially, for co-ordinated political and electoral action, they will not even dent the edifice of neo-liberal capitalism. Little wonder that many on the left who are desperate to remove a truly vicious and reactionary Conservative government turn to Ed Miliband's social democratic Labour Party (for reform at governmental level) or the Green Party (for a progressive alternative and a variety of ethical social initiatives).

Some trade unions are beginning to explore bolder options than simply funding Labour and hoping for the best. In 2009 the trade union created Campaign against Climate Change, working with academics, climate activists and Green campaigners, produced the influential report *One Million Climate Jobs*. Positioning itself firmly as a response to the failures of neoliberal economics it argued that the UK government must create one million "green jobs" – in renewable energy, refitting buildings, public transport, industry and education – in order to emerge from economic crisis with a healthy, sustainable low-carbon economy.[15] On another front, Unite has developed an ambitious programme of "Community Branches" to advise and assist the unemployed in deprived areas, and also to promote the values of trade unionism amongst those who cannot participate because of their exclusion from the world of work. On the national stage the People's Assembly movement, supported by most major trade unions and the Green Party, was successfully launched in May 2013 at a massive event in London addressed by the populist and inspiring leftist writer Owen Jones, Trade Union General Secretaries Len McClusky (Unite) and Mark Serwotka (PCS), the increasingly impressive TUC General Secretary Frances O'Grady, Green MP Caroline Lucas and Tony Benn himself, now an iconic and revered figurehead of the British left. Following this a network of town and city Regional Assemblies have been created as a locus for resistance to savage cuts to local services, and the basis for joined up work between unions, students, welfare campaigners and other activist groups.

Before taking this work forward it would be helpful to clear away some ideological baggage, specifically the sterile arguments between the "revolutionary" and "reformist" left that prevented a united socialist front in the 1970s. Self evidently the policies offered by the Labour left in the 1970s were those of a reformist democratic socialist party. As such they were criticized at the time by the revolutionary left and have been critically assessed since by those who share that perspective. Much of that criticism is valid. In 2010 one intelligent and articulate Marxist commentator rightly judged that Labour's radical 1974 manifesto and its plans for a redistribution of power within business and industry were "... a utopian programme in the strict sense in that no thought had been given to the range of social forces it would be necessary to assemble and mobilize in order that its goals could be achieved, and its accomplishments protected".[16] Nor did the Labour left have a realistic view of the forces – political, economic, institutional – that would frustrate this programme. This does not mean, however, that it was foredoomed or that other revolutionary options (infinitely more utopian) were available. It also sets up an unnecessary barrier between a romantic, undefined upheaval labeled "revolution" and the most radical reform of capitalism that could be envisaged or attempted.

In my view this derives from too rigid definitions of revolution and reform. Reforms within capitalism can be small, piecemeal and inadequate; or they can be more systemic, putting down socio-economic roots and beginning a socialist transformation of key elements of private power and privilege. They can be "revolutionary" in the sense that economic and institutional changes in Tudor and Stuart England laid the foundations of capitalism within the shell of feudalism, or in the sense that continuous pressure from the labour movement in the early 20th century led to the Liberal/Labour creation of the welfare state between 1909 and 1951. The creation of the NHS by Aneurin Bevan, leading and representing generations of socialists, introduced a beating heart of pure socialism into the body of British capitalism that raised the quality of life of millions of working class people and still does. Lenin and the Bolsheviks, on the other hand, after an ill-judged insurrection, crushed political freedom, shut down the genuine socialist democracy of the Soviets, and created a new elite that was parasitic on the working class, and which led eventually to a renewed oligarchic capitalism.[17] Who, in these instances, led and sustained a real revolution?

This is not at all to absolve all reformist strategy and policy.

There are different variants and intensities of socialist reformism at different times, in different circumstances, and with different short and long-term outcomes. The reformism of Aneurin Bevan, Tony Benn or Hugo Chavez is clearly not that of Tony Blair or Bill Clinton, and engagement with any of these should result from a realistic political judgment of the likely results. Most Labour supporting trade union activists in the last hundred years have made those judgments. In the 1970s they shifted back and forth as political possibilities opened and closed. The wave of industrial militancy from 1970 to 1974 was not solely economistic – far from it – but once Labour assumed office on a radical programme it was bound to recede. This was not due to a melodramatic "betrayal" by left union officials but to objective factors such as the initial attraction and delivery of the Social Contract, Labour's receptivity to union concerns, a harsh economic reality that threatened to erode living standards, and loyalty and respect for union leaders like Jack Jones. In short, the radical reformism offered by the Labour left and encapsulated in Labour's Programme 1973 and the AES was, in the given circumstances, the only viable option for those working for achievable social and economic change.

Aneurin Bevan considered that democratic socialism must achieve "passion in action in the pursuit of qualified judgments". To do so means foregoing the emotional satisfaction of advocating revolution without losing the moral fervour required to transform corporate capitalism into a socio-economic system based on a radical redistribution of power and wealth, transparent democracy, participatory economics, and a holistic model of low-carbon growth. This will be a monumental and protracted task, but the conditions for a new radical reformism – for a "British Syriza", however constituted – are now there. From renationalisation of privatised utilities to defending public services to attacking corporate tax avoidance, socialist policies are already popular but they need to be developed and communicated to create a new consensus in British politics.[18] Above all, a radical force or alliance of the left should work in creative partnership with trade unions and with social activists in the student protest movement, UK Uncut, Occupy, anti-Fracking and welfare rights campaigns. It should utilise and develop its own independent social media networks to become a live organisational link between actions outside parliament and delivery inside government. While an open, fluid and democratic structure is important, it is absolutely essential that an incoming radical government, whether formed from a social democratic Labour Party or another left party or a progressive coalition, have an intellectually coherent programme to confront the immense challenges it will face and to shift the centre of political gravity back towards the left.

I have tried to suggest elements of such a programme through discussion of policies that first saw light in the 1970s. The original conception of the National Enterprise Board or a similar body providing strategic direction of industry had great merit. Planning Agreements were valid proposals let down by timid implementation. Benn and the IWC's insistence that public ownership be of a radically different type link today to schemes – seen to good effect in Venezuela's experiment in "21st Century Socialism" – for a new sector of the economy based on workers' self-management and democratic co-operatives. The Lucas Aerospace Alternative Corporate Plan was visionary in prioritising sustainable and socially useful production over short sighted and counter-productive profit accumulation. The Swedish Wage Earners Funds sketched a possible way for society to control investment and redistribute wealth. Other ideas now being considered on the left such as a Basic (or Citizens) Income and a Land Value Tax would add depth to a modern socialist programme. But whatever policies are put to the electorate the left will have to confront and overcome the main obstacle to applying them – the international financial rules of globalised neo-liberalism. I do not see how this can be done other than at the European and international level in alliance with other national left parties. Without fundamentally altering these rules (through, at the least, a new Bretton Woods Agreement, reform of the GATT, and an international Transaction Tax on capital movements) a reformist socialist government will be constrained in what it can achieve even if it had radical economic policies it wished to implement.

This new "coalition of redistribution",[19] whatever it may eventually be called, should ideally encompass the best of the Labour tradition of Nye Bevan and Tony Benn but not romanticise and repeat their every policy or position. This book has highlighted Benn's crucial and at times heroic role in the challenge presented by Labour in the 1970s to the British establishment, and yet we must accept that this challenge failed. One reason for that failure was an overestimation of the traditional male working class trade union movement which in its glory – in the Miners' strikes of the 1970s and 1980s and at Saltly Gates – could turn the world upside down, but nonetheless failed to renovate its ideology and its strategies when faced with potential new allies amongst feminist, gay and environmental movements, and new enemies on the right who planned to destroy its power-bases and its legal protections. In the 1970s and 1980s there existed an enormous, and missed, opportunity to forge a "red-green" alliance between the labour movement and the libertarian, progressive ecological left that only a few socialists such as Ken Coates perceived and valued. The Labour left and its union allies therefore entered the 1980s alone and went down to a tragic and severe defeat. In this respect Tony Benn may have been, as Donald Sassoon claimed, "one of the last representatives of a distinguished if somewhat insular English radical tradition doomed to disappear".[20]

The massive, spontaneous outpouring of grief and respect for Benn upon his death in March 2014 suggests it has not quite disappeared. And in any case, the inspiring legacy remains. At its best the British labour movement in the 1970s demonstrated a boldness and clarity in challenging the basis of a profit driven capitalism that should resonate to this day. It was the trade unions who led worker occupations like UCS, who threw back the Industrial Relations Act and brought down a Tory government. It was Labour who sought to achieve a fundamental redistribution of wealth and power to working people and their families. It was the wider left who stood up for Salvador Allende, Michael Manley and Irish Catholics. It was Benn who fought the IMF within government with every ministerial resource he possessed. And it was Benn who urged the workers of Lucas Aerospace to develop their own Corporate Plan that put collective creativity and meeting the social needs of the sick and disabled over making money from war production.

Nowhere was the impetus to a more civilised society better expressed than in the Lucas Aerospace Combine's own report on its work in the 1970s, which proudly states "a socialist industrial strategy rejects competitive success as an overriding objective. Instead we must reassert that the objective of a socialist industrial strategy is to match productive capacity and human energies and skills to social needs under democratic control".[21] The British left will continue to debate policy and strategy but this, ultimately, is the essence of its challenge to the obscene wealth inequality, environmental destruction and moral corruption of corporate capitalism, and of its ambition to "remould it nearer to the Heart's Desire".[22]

References

Introduction – History for the Losers

1. Dominic Sandbrook, "Miliband's Marxist father and the real reason he wants to drag us back to the nightmare 70s", *Daily Mail*, 26th September 2013. Sandbrook lowered himself even further when, in the *Daily Mail*, 15th March 2014, his obituary of Tony Benn claimed that if Benn had his way in the 1970s he would have turned the UK into North Korea.

2. *The Sun*, 29th September 2013.

3. James Thomas, *Popular Newspapers, the Labour Party, and British Politics*, Routledge, 2005, p.81

4. Donald Sassoon, *One Hundred Years of Socialism: The West European Left in the Twentieth Century*, I.B Tauris, 1996, p.451

5. 3rd Report of the Treasury and Civil Service Committee, Monetary Policy, HMSO, 1981, referenced in Geoff Hodgson, *Labour at the Crossroads*, Martin Roberston, 1981, p.175

6. Alex Nunns, "Thatcher didn't save the economy, she wrecked it – and we're still paying the price", *Red Pepper*, April 2013

7. Nunns, Ibid, *Red Pepper*.

8. Alan Bailey, *Not all the Bad Old Days*, IPPR, 7th February 2013, www.ippr.org

9. Quoted in Kiran Moodley, "Thatcher's greatest legacy: the rewriting of history", *New Statesman*, 16th April 2013

10. BBC Prime Ministers and Politics Timeline, http://www.bbc.co.uk/history/british/launch_tl_politics_pm.shtml

11. BBC, Ibid

12. Philip Larkin, *Selected Letters*, Faber & Faber, 1993.

13. *History of Modern Britain*, BBC1, first broadcast 22nd May-19th June 2007. In some respects Marr's amiable liberalism make his omissions and distortions on the 1970s more insidious than a straightforward attack by the *Spectator*.

14. Danny Dorling, *Fair Play*, Policy Press, 2011.

15. High Pay Commission, Final Report, 2011.
    http://highpaycentre.org/files/Cheques_with_Balances.pdf

16. Trish Lorenz, *That '70s Showcase*, Financial Times, 26th April 2013.

17. A purely personal and subjective note. I was born in August 1962 and experienced the 1970s as a 7-16 year old in Camden Town and Haverstock Hill, North London. My own memories of those years are in Technicolor – Marine Ices, the fair on Hampstead Heath, *The Tomorrow People*, *Tiswas*, *Space: 1999*, Sweet, Suzi Quatro, *The Spy Who Loved Me*, Camden Lock and *Dark They Were, and Golden Eyed* sci-fi/underground bookshop in Soho. I have no personal recollection of the Winter of Discontent at all.

18. Tim Jackson, New Economic Foundation, Measure of Domestic Progress Report
    http://www.neweconomics.org/publications/entry/chasing-progress

19. Chris Snowdon, *Was 1976 really the best year?*, IEA, December 2013, www.iea.org.uk.

Chapter One: The Big Flame

1. February 1974 Labour Party Manifesto, Archive of Labour Party Manifestos,
   http://www.labour-party.org.uk/manifestos/1974/Feb/1974-feb-labour-manifesto.shtml

2. Tony Cliff, *The Labour Party: A Marxist History*, Bookmarks, 1988, p.314

3. Quoted in Tudor Jones, *Remaking the Labour Party*, Routledge, 1996, p.92

4. See Roger Seifert's excellent biography of Bert Ramelson, *Revolutionary Communist at Work: A Political Biography of Bert Ramelson*, Lawrence and Wisart, 2012, for an in-depth study of the role of the Communist Party at that time and its

critical stance on the Social Contract.

5. Quoted in John A. Walker, *Left Shift: Radical Art in 1970s Britain*, I.B Tauris, 2002, and Ibid, p.2

6. There are many definitions of working class politics and culture, one of the best from the Marxist cultural theorist Raymond Williams – *"It is not Proletarian Art, or council houses, or a particular use of language: it is, rather, the basic collective idea and the institutions, manners, habits of thought and intentions which proceed from this"* (Williams, *Culture and Society* 1780-1950, Anchor, p.544)

7. Michael Foot, *Aneurin Bevan: 1945-60*, Faber Finds, 2010 (1973), p.60-102

8. *We Won't Pay: Women's struggle on Tower Hill*, Big Flame, 1970-84, wordpress.com, May 2009.
http://bigflameuk.files.wordpress.com/2009/05/tower-all.pdf

9. Peter Shapley, *Social Housing and Tenant Participation*,
http://www.historyandpolicy.org/papers/policy-paper-71.html

10. Colin Ward, *Hidden History of Housing*, September 2005.
http://www.historyandpolicy.org/papers/policy-paper-25.html

11. *Hackney: Cradle for Subversives*,
http://hackneyhistory.wordpress.com/timeline/

12. George McKay, *Radical Gardening: politics, idealism and rebellion in the garden*, Frances Lincoln, 2011, p.121-22, which brings out the radical implications and challenge of the British allotment, organic and guerrilla gardening movements, in the sense of re-colonising private and public space for non commercial ends.

13. The legacy of the Levellers, the Ranters and the Diggers during the period 1640-60 was disinterred and presented sympathetically in the most important work of British history of the 1970s – Christopher Hill's *The World Turned Upside Down* (1972). Hill's book was part of a revolution in

British historiography. With E.P Thompson's *The Making of the English Working Class* and Eric Hobsbawm's studies of the 19th century and the Industrial Revolution it established Marxism as a central tool in the study of history in British schools and universities. From Thatcher to Gove one of the right's key projects has been to erase it and replace it with purely narrative history emphasising events, dates, "great men" and British Imperial triumph.

14. Walker, Ibid, p.104
15. Alistair Livingstone, *Goodbye to London radical art and politics in the 70s,*
    http://Greengalloway.blogspot.co.uk.
    August 17th, 2012. Accessed 10th October 2013.
16. Astrid Proll, Introduction to *Goodbye to London*, Hatje Cantz, 2010, p.8-11
17. Alex Comfort, *More Joy of Sex*, 1973; quoted in David Goodway, *Anarchist Seeds Beneath the Snow*, 2012, Kindle Edition.
18. The autobiographies of Tariq Ali and Christopher Hitchens include interesting vignettes of temporary collisions and alliances in the late 1960s and early 1970s between Marxist groups like the IMG and IS and working class trade union activists. Jim Higgins' fascinating and humorous book on the origins of the SWP, *More Years for the Locust*, reports hundreds of union activists at *Socialist Worker* rallies in the early 1970s (most of these would later be driven away by excess sectarianism). Ralph Miliband's *The State in Capitalist Society* (1969) was one of the few works by a major Marxist theorist that engaged with concrete issues of institutional power and how it functioned. Whilst it is difficult to trace the effect of academic work on political struggle, many personal memoirs of the time reflect his influence on left thinking.
19. For data on women in the workforce and female union density in the 1970s see Chris Wrigley, "Women in the

Labour Market and in the Unions", in *The High Tide of British Trade Unionism: Trade Unions and Industrial Politics 1964-79*, edited by John McIlroy, Nina Fishman, and Alan Campbell, Merlin, 2007.

20. Jim Higgins, *More Years for the Locust*, Unkant, 1997, p.139

Chapter Two: The Socialist Challenge

1. See Jack Jones, *Union Man*, Collins, 1986, Chapter 10. It is worth remembering that two men savagely attacked by the *Daily Mail* – Jack Jones and Ralph Miliband – both put their lives on the line to defeat fascism before and during the Second World War, while the *Mail* strongly supported Mosley's Blackshirts and appeasement of Nazi Germany.

2. *The Guardian*, Obituary Jimmy Reid, 11th August 2010

3. Immanuel Ness and Dario Azzellini, *Ours to Master and to Own: Workers' Control from the Commune to the Present*, Haymarket Books, 2011, p.290-92

4. Dave Sherry, *Occupy! A short history of workers' occupations*, Bookmarks, 2010, p.121

5. Ness and Azzelini, Ibid, p.285

6. Tony Cliff, *The Crisis: Social Contract or Socialism*, Pluto, 1975, p.151

7. Chris Harman, *The Fire Last Time: 1968 and after*, Bookmarks, 1988, p.246

8. Paul Foot, *The Vote: How it was won and how it was undermined*, Penguin, 2005, p.371. Foot's book, although written from the perspective of the SWP and critical of the reformism of the Labour Party, is remarkably fair to the efforts of (some of) the Labour Party and Government of 1974-79 to push that reformism as far as circumstances would allow. His criticisms of its actions and inactions are trenchant and valid although in my opinion they mistakenly presuppose that other non-specified "revolutionary" strategies were viable at the time.

9. Chris Hemming, *Growth of the Left within the Labour Party*

during the 1970s,
http://www.labour-history.org.uk/support_files/labour%20
and%20left.PDF

10. For an insight into the intensely conservative and often corrupt culture of some of the old right-wing local Labour parties, see the first chapters of Peter Tatchell, *The Battle for Bermondsey*, Heretic Books, 1983.

11. Hemming, Ibid, p.3

12. Stuart Holland, *The Socialist Challenge*, Quartet Books, 1975

13. Department for Economic Affairs (DEA), *The Task Ahead*, 1969

14. Stuart Holland, *Strategy for Socialism*, Spokesman, 1975, p.15

15. Tony Benn, 1973 Labour Party Conference, 1st-5th October 1973.

16. Stuart Holland, *Demythologising Old Labour*, The Spokesman, 2010, p.26.

17. Michael Hatfield, *The House the Left Built*, Gollancz, 1978, p.199

18. Leo Panitch and Colin Leys, *The End of Parliamentary Socialism: From New Left to New Labour*, Verso, 1997, p.83-84. A superb examination of Labour's trajectory from the 1970s to the 1990s to which I am very indebted.

Chapter Three: Workers' Control

1. Hatfield, Ibid, p.67

2. Tony Benn, *Towards a Socialist Industrial Policy*, 1971, quoted in Hatfield, p.79

3. Andrew Cumbers, *Reclaiming Public Ownership*, Zed Books, 2012, p.15

4. Eric Hobsbawm, Review, New Statesman, 1973

5. Tony Benn, *Arguments for Socialism*, Penguin, 1980, p.66. Benn's book is a much under-appreciated political testament and a key document in understanding the positions he took in the 1970s and 1980s.

6. Ken Coates, *Socialists and the Labour Party*, Spokesman

Pamphlet No 52, 1973, p.2

7. Coates, Ibid, p.8

8. Coates, Ibid, p.20

9. Labour Party Conference, 1973, quoted in "Whatever Happened to Industrial Democracy?" in *What Went Wrong?: Explaining the fall of the Labour Government*, edited by Ken Coates, Spokesman Books, p.126

10. Dorril and Ramsay, *Smear! Wilson and the Secret State*, Grafton, 1991, p.281. Dorril and Ramsay's definitive work on the secret state and its political agenda in the 1960s and 1970s was, in the opinion of *The Times Literary Supplement*, "Easily the best and most detailed account of the Wilson and related plots". The investigative journalist Phillip Knightley said "It reveals the secret wellsprings of power in Britain". It is one of the essential works on British politics of the era, and its attention to detail and sourcing of hidden and damning evidence is forensic. Naturally it is out of print and hardly ever referenced. I have drawn heavily on it for these parts of the narrative.

11. *Tony Benn and the IWC Debate: An Account of the Institute for Workers' Control meeting at the Labour Party Conference, November 1974* – IWC Pamphlet No 45. The pamphlets and discussion of the IWC are recommended for all who see Labour history through a misleading Old Labour/New Labour dichotomy. New Labour was essentially a rebranded version of traditional Labourite social democracy as practised by Hugh Gaitskell, Harold Wilson and Denis Healey (i.e Old Labour) whereas what is commonly presented as Old Labour (the Bennite left and its allies) was far more imaginative and experimental in seeking democratic solutions to the problems of corporate capitalism.

12. Benn, *IWC Pamphlet No 45*, p.25

13. Christopher Andrew, *Defence of the Realm: The Authorised History of MI5*, Penguin, 2009, p.590.

Chapter Four: Low Intensity Operationsv

1. Peter Wright, *Spycatcher*, Viking, 1987, p.360. See also Stephen Dorril, *The Silent Conspiracy: Inside the Intelligence Services in the 1980s*, Mandarin, 1993, "Appendix: MI5 Organisational Structure 1981-83", which was very similar to its structure in the mid 1970s.

2. Andrew, Ibid, P.596-97

3. Dorill and Ramsay, Ibid, p.265

4. Dorrill and Ramsay, Ibid, p.266

5. Frank Kitson, *Low Intensity Operations*, Faber Finds, 2010 (1971).

6. *Socialist Worker*, Issue 2063, 2007. For the entire story of the British State's collusion with and covert direction of unionist death squads in Northern Ireland see Anne Cadwallader's *Lethal Allies: British Collusion in Ireland*, Mercier Press, 2013. On the back of his record in Northern Ireland Kitson went on to become Commander-in-Chief of UK Land Forces and Aide-de-Camp General to the Queen.

7. "Wilson, MI5 and the Rise of Thatcher", *Lobster* 11, April 1986.

8. Ralph Miliband, "The Coup in Chile", *Socialist Register*, 1973, reprinted in *Revolution and Class Struggle: A Reader in Marxist Politics*, Harper Collins, 1977, p.435.

9. Dorill and Ramsay, Ibid, p.267 for more on GB75. Oddly enough I have a vague personal connection to this affair. In the 1970s my dad, despite his left-wing politics, became a driver and general fixer for a property magnate, Michael Carlton, who dabbled in the shadowy world of the Clermont Club, an exclusive preserve in Berkeley Square for high stakes gamblers and far right businessmen. He often drove Carlton and David Stirling to the Club and overheard them discuss GB75 and related plots in the back of the car. On one occasion he was given an unmarked package and told to deliver it to the MI5 Registry in Curzon St. In his self-

published autobiography he wrote about leaving school at 15 to sample the Soho jazz clubs of the 1950s, working in the building trade of the 1960s, and encounters with property speculators and faded aristocrats in the West End of the 1970s (see Ted Medhurst, *Charlie Potatoes*, Medhurst Books, 2009).

10. *Lobster* 11, Ibid.

11. Paul Foot, *Who Framed Colin Wallace?*, Pan, 1990, p.79

12. John Pilger, *Hidden Agendas*, Vintage, 1998, p.516

13. Duncan Campbell, "The Heathrow Manoeuvres", from Undercurrents 11
http://www.duncancampbell.org/content/undercurrents
Accessed 5th November 2013

14. Andy Beckett, *When the Lights Went Out: What Really Happened to Britain in the Seventies*, Faber & Faber, 2008.

15. *Morning Star*, 28th January 1974

16. *Daily Mail*, 20th September 2008

17. February 1974 Labour Party Manifesto, Archive of Labour Party Manifestos,
http://www.labour-party.org.uk/manifestos/1974/Feb/1974-feb-labour-manifesto.shtml

Chapter Five: Social Contract

1. Although Labour won the February 1974 General Election it did so on a lower overall vote than it had lost in 1970. The Tories also lost vote share, as voters looked to alternatives such as the nationalist parties (see Cliff, *The Labour Party: A Marxist History*, Ibid, p. 319). Although this might indicate that the wave of industrial and political radicalism of the early 1970s was not a universal phenomenon (as, of course, it wasn't) and could not be relied on to sustain a more revolutionary challenge to British capitalism, Cliff draws the opposite conclusion. In reality it was the lack of a widespread socialist consensus in society that restrained Benn and the left in Parliament, not the other way around.

2. Labour Party October 1974 General Election Manifesto
    http://www.labour-party.org.uk/manifestos/1974/Oct/1974-
    oct-labour-manifesto.shtml

3. Jones, Ibid, p.279-80

4. Kenneth O. Morgan, *Michael Foot*, Harper Perennial, 2007,
    p.250. By far the best book on the life, politics and writings
    of a literate and humane man, who in 1969 addressed a
    Morning Star rally and called for the breaking down of
    "sectarian walls" on the left, as well as hailing Marxism as "a
    great creed of human liberation" (Ibid, p.262).

5. Jones, Ibid, p.295.

6. Will Hutton, *The State We're In*, Vintage, 1996, p.132-36

7. Michael Barratt Brown, "The Record of the 1974-79 Labour
    Government: The Growth and Distribution of Income and
    Wealth", in *What Went Wrong*, Ibid, p39-50.

8. Noam Chomsky, *Hopes and Prospects*, Penguin, 2011, p.97.
    Not for the first or only time Chomsky is more lucid and
    insightful about international globalisation and economic
    policy making than most professional economists and
    political scientists.

9. The sympathetic (minority) response within the CP to the
    Social Contract was centred on the economists Dave Purdey,
    Mike Prior and Pat Devine. They argued that a "socialist
    incomes policy" would allow space for more systemic struc-
    tural reforms that, unlike annual pay increases, would not
    be small finite gains. The advocates of this approach were
    precursors of the Euro Communists within the CP and were
    critical of the "economism" of the Industrial Department led
    by Bert Ramelson (See "Notes on the Communist Party and
    Industrial Politics", John McIlroy, in *The High Tide of British
    Trade Unionism, Trade Unions and Industrial Politics 1964-79,
    Merlin*, 1999). In "Pay Policies and Sacred Cows", *The
    Leveller*, February 1979, in the midst of the Winter of
    Discontent, Purdey wrote "The current tendency to climb

aboard the bandwagon of disillusionment with the social contract, and to identify progress with every fresh pay dispute is sadly mistaken. It is leading away from a coherent socialist strategy for Britain". The CP's leading historian Eric Hobsbawm, who supported Purdey's line, had already written of the lack of a long term strategy on the British left. In his influential 1978 essay "The Forward March of Labour Halted?" he suggested that for all the scale and drama of the upsurge of industrial militancy in the early 1970s, the strikes which dominated it (the struggle against the Industrial Relation Act excepted) had mostly conventional aims – i.e the winning of better pay and terms and conditions. In this, he argued, they reflected the sectionalism and economism of the British trade union movement. In my view Hobsbawm underestimated the full range of industrial actions of the period, and does not seem to have engaged at all with the occupations and sit-ins of the early 1970s or the concept of "encroachment" on capitalist relations of production offered by the Workers' Control movement. This may be because, as a Communist, he considered "actually existing socialism" should be solely State run. His essay has been represented as an argument for Neil Kinnock's subsequent abandonment of socialist policies. This is unfair given that a) it was written even before Labour's defeat in 1979 let alone the inter-party battles of the early 1980s, and b) Hobsbawm explicitly repudiated the "Third Way" and New Labour in *Marxism Today*'s one off retrospective in 1998. In reality, Hobsbawm was arguing for neither right-wing defeatism nor sectarian "workerism" but an open minded engagement with social movements and demographic trends within British society, without which the socialist left would remain stuck in an historic cul-de-sac.

10. Andy Beckett, *Pinochet in Piccadilly*, Faber & Faber, 2002, p.174

11. Dominic Simpson, "Centreprise – the radical past of a much missed Hackney Institution", *Hackney Citizen*, 12th September 2013

    http://hackneycitizen.co.uk/2013/09/12/centerprise-history/

12. Beckett, ibid, p.154

13. Tony Benn, *Against the Tide: Diaries 1973-76*, Arrow, p.136

Chapter Six: Power Sharing

1. Benn, Ibid, p.118

2. *The Times*, 17th June 1974.

3. Panitch and Leys, Ibid, p.90

4. *Lobster* 11, Ibid

5. Robert Fisk, *Point of No Return*, Andrew Deutsch, 1975, p.87-88

6. In the 1950s there were 50,000 shipbuilders on the Clyde alone, and British shipbuilders made half the ships in the world. In 1974 despite stiff competition from Japan and Korea they had orders booked four years ahead. There were underlying problems with integrating modern technology and demarcation disputes that could have been resolved if the workforce were treated as partners. Public ownership could have achieved this but British Shipbuilders was a huge and tragic missed opportunity. Run as a public corporation by central government it simply downsized and focused on short-term contracts. It started to commit suicide in 1983 when the Conservative government sold off its naval yards. By 1987 it was employing 5,000 people on the Clyde and two yards on Wearside whereas ten years before it had employed 35,000. In 1988 the Sunderland yards were closed and flattened to become an Enterprise Zone (see David Bowen, "Britain Misses the Boat", *The Independent*, 4th September 1994). As this happened there was a massive loss of cohesion and morale in the shipyard communities of the North East. Nothing captures this history and its sad closure as well as

the haunting songs of the industrial folk band The Unthanks, especially their *Vol. 3, Songs from the Shipyards*. In the sleeve notes Adrian McNally writes "Impressions and accounts of our industrial past often tread the line between proud memories and rose tinted glasses; between the respect we have for the people who worked hard and the danger of glorifying their lives as honest, decent and proper; between describing them as great days and remembering that they were tough and dangerous days; between the pride for what the workers achieved and the reality of the wealth it created being siphoned away from their communities. And finally, the emotional complexity for those communities of having created something great, only to be completely deserted when the going got tough". Or, as a senior civil servant told Sir Robert Atkinson, Chairman of British Shipbuilders, in the 1980s, "Margaret wants rid of shipbuilding. Remember that".

7. Morgan, Ibid, Chapters 8 & 9 for a detailed and balanced defence of Foot's work at the DoE and his commitment to working with the trade unions.

8. Morgan, Ibid, p.295

9. Tony Blair, Introduction to the Labour Government White Paper "Fairness at Work", 1998, which he admitted left UK employment law in this state. He did not mean it as a criticism.

10. Sassoon, Ibid, p.707

11. Sassoon, Ibid, p.709

12. Robin Blackburn, *A Visionary Pragmatist*, 22 December 2005. http://www.counterpunch.org/2005/12/22/a-visionary-pragmatist/

Chapter Six: A Cold Coup

1. Benn, Ibid, p.127

2. Panitch and Leys, Ibid, p.99

3. Ness and Azzelini, Ibid, p.295

4. As reported by Michael Meacher in "Whitehall's Short Way With Democracy", in *What Went Wrong*, Ibid, p.180

5. Hatfield, Ibid, p.233

6. Hatfield, Ibid, p.236

7. See Panitch and Leys, p.95-97, for a summary of Benn's report and its reception.

8. *State Intervention in Industry: A Workers Inquiry*, Russell Press, 1980, p.36. In all the academic and professional commentary on Labour's industrial strategy in the mid 1970s, I have not come across a better, more informed or cogently argued analysis of its attempted implementation that this, produced by workers and activists in the Coventry, Liverpool, Newcastle and North Tyneside Trades Councils.

9. Harold Wilson, *Final Term*, Michael Joseph, 1979, quoted in Simon James, *British Government: A Reader in Policy Making*, Routledge, 1997, p.122

10. Benn, Ibid, p.212-218, for the discussion in Cabinet and what appears Benn's initial over-estimation of what he had secured. The White Paper contained more of the Working Group's draft than did the final Industry Act, but it is curious that Benn and Heffer's first response was very different to their critical judgement once they had taken it all on board. This seems to be because it was weakened still further in Committee stages before it became statute. Stuart Holland later wrote that "one had the situation where virtually all the Labour members of that Committee were voting for Labour's Programme, and they were outvoted by the Government and one or two Labour members siding with the Tories and Liberals" (Holland, *Labour Leader*, May 1977).

11. Hodgson, Ibid, p.97

12. Panitch and Leys, Ibid, p.102

13. Ian Gilmour, *Inside Right*, Quartet, 1977, p.211

14. Brian Wheeler, *Wilson Plot: The Secret Tapes*, BBC News.org ,

9th March, 2006

15. Lord Chalfont, *Could Britain be Headed for a Military Coup?*, The Times, 5th August 1974

Chapter Seven: Children of the Revolution

1. *The Portuguese Revolution 1974-75*, libcom.org, 2006. http://libcom.org/history/1974-1975-the-portuguese-revolution Accessed 16th October 2013.
2. Cheryl L. King, *Michael Manley and Democratic Socialism*, Resource, 2003, p.43
3. King, Ibid, p.45
4. Walker, Ibid, p.119, p.142, and p.120
5. Dave Haslan, *Young Hearts, Run Free*, Harper Perennial, 2005, p.220
6. I would argue that Disco was more politically progressive than Punk and more odious to far right sentiment. The violent language and imagery of Punk could be and was co-opted by street level fascist thugs. Disco was far harder to reconcile with racist bigotry, in fact impossible, as the far right recognised. In 1979 the BNP's youth magazine *The Young Nationalist* complained that *"Disco and its melting pot pseudo-philosophy must be fought or Britain's streets will be full of black worshipping soul boys"* (quoted in Haslan, p.156).
7. Michael Bracewell, *England Is Mine*, Flamingo, 1998, p.194
8. With the passage of time it is clear that Moorcock and J.G Ballard were the outstanding English novelists of the 1970s, both of whom emerged from the experimental *New Worlds* SF magazine of the 1960s. Whilst neither were totally invisible to the arbiters of literary excellence (Moorcock's *The Condition of Muzak* won the Guardian Fiction Prize in 1977) they were certainly on the margins of respectability. Far beyond those margins, one of the most significant products of British popular art in the 1970s – the weekly comic

2000AD, launched in 1977 – was simply off the spectrum of critical consideration, despite its originality and dizzying creativity. Its most popular character, Judge Dredd, is now a British fictional literary icon on a par with Sherlock Holmes, Tarzan and James Bond. The brutal and witty Dredd stories were far ahead of mainstream fiction in satirising the authoritarian politics and cultural degeneration of technologically advanced corporate capitalism. *2000AD* paved the way for the work of great British writers such as Alan Moore (*V for Vendetta, From Hell, The League of Extroadinary Gentlemen*) and Bryan Talbot (*Luther Arkwright, Heart of Empire, Alice in Sunderland*) whose work, because it is presented in the medium of Graphic Novels, occupies the same position in regard to the contemporary British literary scene as Moorcock's did in the 1970s.

9. Sheila Rowbotham and Jeffrey Weeks, *The Personal and Sexual Politics of Edward Carpenter and Havelock Ellis*, Pluto Press, 1977, p.23. For Rowbotham this was a brief sketch at what would eventually be her full length, prize winning biography *Edward Carpenter: A Life of Liberty and Love* (Verso, 2008) a superlative and ground breaking book on a long neglected late 19th/early 20th century ethical socialist of great influence on the early Labour Party.

10. Ian Townson, *The Brixton Fairies and the South London Gay Community Centre 1974-76*,
    http://www.urban75.org/blog/the-brixton-fairies-and-the-south-london-gay-community-centre-brixton-1974-6/
    Accessed 11th December 2013.

11. Townson, Ibid

12. Benn, Ibid, p.518

13. John McIlroy, "Always Outnumbered, Always Outgunned: The Trotskyists and the Trade Unions", in *The High Tide of British Trade Unionism: 1964-1979*, Ibid, p.280

14. Higgins, Ibid, p.191

15. Referenced in E.P Thompson, *The Poverty of Theory*, Merlin, 1978, p.36

16. Perry Anderson, "Components of the National Culture", *Student Power*, Penguin, 1969, p.225. It is possible that Anderson came to realise that he and Nairn had gone too far in their arguments in the 1960s and in their dismissive response to E.P Thompson. Anderson's later book *Arguments within English Marxism* (1980) makes some apology for that and is a sustained attempt to engage critically but positively with the entire corpus of Thompson's work, calling Thompson *"our finest socialist writer today – certainly in England, possibly in Europe"*.

17. E.P Thompson, "The Peculiarities of the English", *The Socialist Register*, ed. Ralph Miliband and John Saville, No 2, 1965.

18. Anderson, Ibid, p.215

19. See Anderson, "The Limits and Possibilities of Trade Union Action", *The Incompatibles: Trade Union Militancy and the Consensus*, Penguin, 1967.

20. Perry Anderson, *Considerations on Western Marxism*, Verso, 1979, p.79 (NLB 1976)

21. Anderson, Ibid, p.80.

Chapter Eight: Useful Work v. Useful Toil

1. *The Guardian*, Obituary Brian Crozier, 9th August 2012

2. Dorill and Ramsay, Ibid, p.271

3. Benn, Ibid, p237

4. *Financial Times*, 16th October 1974

5. David Kynaston, *The City of London: A Club No More 1945-2000*, Pimlico, 2002, p.508

6. Benn, Ibid, p.247

7. Chancellor, Memorandum to Cabinet, "Public Expenditure Priorities", 30/10/1974

8. Quoted in Edmund Dell, *A Hard Pounding*, OUP, 1991, p.121

9. Benn, Ibid, p.263

10. Hilary Wainwright and Matt Elliott, *The Lucas Plan: A new trade unionism in the making*, Allison and Busby, 1982, p.83

11. Benn, Ibid, p.162

12. Wainwright and Elliott, Ibid, p.10

13. William Morris, *Useful Work v. Useless Toil*, Penguin Great Ideas (2013), first published 1888. Morris's work and thought, especially his development of Marxism to encompass a cultural critique of commercialised capitalism and the alienation of workers from the work process, continues to stay fresh and grow more and more relevant. For the definitive personal biography see Fiona McCarthy's *William Morris*, Faber & Faber, 1994, but for the most intellectually rich, inspiring examination of his political life and significance, see E.P Thompsons' classic *William Morris: Romantic to Revolutionary*, Merlin, reprinted 2011, originally published 1955, revised 1976.

14. *The Guardian*, Obituary Sir Anthony Part, 11th December 1991

Chapter Nine: Alternative Economic Strategy

1. Benn, Ibid, p.297

2. Benn, Ibid, p.329

3. Secretary of State for Industry, Memorandum to Cabinet, "A Choice of Economic Policies", February 25th, 1975.

4. Kaldor had seen the intellectual threat to Keynesian economics and the shoddy argumentative base of Friedman's monetarism as early as 1970. In "The New Monetarism", *Lloyds Bank Review*, No 97, he warned that major monetary institutions were falling to "pseudo-scientism", and that *"...the research staff of the IMF, or at least the majority of them, are secret, if not open, Friedmanites"*.

5. Bob Rowthorn, "The Politics of the Alternative Economic Strategy", *Marxism Today*, January 1981, for a rigorous

analysis and defence of the AES from the perspective of the early 1980s, in which he argues that "The very act of creating and developing the AES is an important exercise in self-education for socialists. It helps them to think coherently and forces them to consider how various reforms can be welded into a unified whole".

6. Nicholas Kaldor, "A Model of Economic Growth"
   http://www.cultureofdoubt.net/download/docs_cod/kaldor%20economic%20growth%201957.pdf

7. Lewis Minkin, *The Contentious Alliance: Trade Unions and the Labour Party*, EUP, 1992, p.17

8. Secretary of State for Industry, Memorandum to Cabinet, summary at PREM 16/341, National Archives, Gov.uk

9. Greg Philo, *Really Bad News*, London 1982, p.105, quoted in Panitch and Leys, Ibid, p.92

10. Panitch and Leys, Ibid, p.92

11. Dorril and Ramsay, Ibid, p.279. In July 1975 Benn's daughter Melissa made a call from Benn's office phone in the family home. Later she picked up another phone and heard her earlier conversation played back. There were numerous instances like this at this time (Benn, Ibid, p.424).

12. Dorril and Ramsay, Ibid, p.253-54

13. Andrew, Ibid, note 30, p.977

14. Benn, Ibid, p.294

15. Kynaston, Ibid, p.533

Chapter Ten: Commitments with the City

1. John Medhurst and Enrico Tortolano, "The Future of the European Union: A Critical Trade Union View", *Journal of Contemporary European Research*, Vol 7, No4, 2009

2. Medhurst & Tortolano, Ibid

3. Benn, Ibid, p.346

4. Michael Cockerell, *How Britain first fell for Europe*, BBC News.org, June 4, 2005

5. Benn, Ibid, p.390

6. Benn, Ibid, p 389-395. The narrative of the removal of Benn and the emotionally intense meetings between him and Wilson on 9th and 10th June 1975 is drawn from Benn's *Diaries* and so is from his perspective only. However, no subsequent commentator or source has ever contested its basic veracity.

7. Panitch and Leys, Ibid, p.105

8. Quoted in Kynaston, Ibid, p.521

9. Quoted in Kynaston, Ibid, p.535

10. Lucas Aerospace, the company, retained its friends in high places. After his retirement in 1976 Sir Anthony Part, the DoI Permanent Secretary who had done so much to block Benn's attempts to create workers' co-ops and encourage plans like that of the Lucas Aerospace Combine, became a Director of EMI, Debenhams, Metal Box, Savoy Hotels – and Lucas Aerospace. He left the civil service in June 1976 and took up his Directorship with LA in October 1976 (*State Intervention in Industry: A Workers' Inquiry*, Ibid, p.106). When the final LA Alternative Corporate Plan reached Secretary of State for Industry Gerald Kaufman in late 1976, Kaufman, heavily briefed by his officials, replied "I have been firmly of the view that the proper place for the examination of your ideas must be, at least initially, within Lucas Aerospace". This was written after the company, whose Board by then included Sir Anthony Part, had refused to negotiate on the plan (Ibid, p.104).

11. Hodgson, Ibid, p.102

12. Judith Hart, *The Guardian*, 1st July 1975

Chapter Eleven: The moment of defeat

1. Tristram Hunt, *The forward march of Labour restarted?*, IPPR Vol 18, November 2011.

2. Pilger, Ibid, p.416

3. Jones, Ibid, p. 296
4. Jones, Ibid, p.299
5. Benn, Ibid, p.415
6. Ian Birchall, *Building "The smallest Mass Party in the world"*, *SWP 1951-79*, *www.marxists.org/history/etol/revhist/otherdox/smp/smp3.html*
7. Hodgson, Ibid, p.110
8. Quoted in Haslan, Ibid, p.203
9. Panitch and Leys, Ibid, p.108
10. Kathleen Burk, "Symposium: 1976 IMF Crisis", *Contemporary Record*, November 1989, p.43, from Kynaston, p.827
11. TUC, *Report of Special Congress*, 19th June 1976, p.39
12. John Maloney, "The Treasury and the New Cambridge School in the 1970s", *Cambridge Journal of Economics*, Vol 36, Issue 4, p.27-28
13. Labour Party Conference, September 1976
14. Labour Party Conference, September 1976
15. Quoted in Andrew Glyn and John Harrison, *The British Economic Disaster*, Pluto, 1980, p.97
16. Chancellor, Memoradum to Cabinet, "IMF Negotiations", 22nd November 1976
17. Chancellor, Memorandum to Cabinet, Ibid
18. Secretary of State for Energy, Memorandum to Cabinet, "The Real Choices Facing the Cabinet", 29th November 1976
19. Secretary of State for Energy, Memorandum to Cabinet, Ibid
20. Alan Travis, "IMF crisis forced Labour to consider scrapping Polaris", *The Guardian*, 29th December 2006.
21. Travis, Ibid, *Guardian.*
22. Benn, Ibid, p.672
23. Benn, Ibid, 679
24. Quoted in Panitch and Leys, Ibid, p.128
25. Kynaston, Ibid, p.551
26. Denis Healey, *The Time of My Life*, Politico's, 2006, p.401-02
27. Benn, Ibid, p.119

Conclusion: Passion in action

1. The conservative historian Paul Johnson, in a readable and thought provoking history of the 20th century that undermines itself with specious arguments the further it progresses, nevertheless correctly identifies "...*the return to authority which characterised the transition from the 1970s to the 1980s*" (Johnson, *Modern Times*, Phoenix Giant, 1999, p.703). Johnson speaks for many conservatives who disparage the 1970s not for particular economic reasons but because it was a time in which "authority" was questioned and defied.

2. There was a respectable argument for the Social Contract in the early and mid 1970s and it has been made by its chief advocates Jack Jones and Michael Foot. Foot's lecture, "A Contract for the 1980s", delivered at the Royal Institute of Public Administration, Cardiff, November 1982, included a robust case for the Social Contract of the 1970s, at least in its early stages. His view deserves airing: "My conclusion is, contrary to the general assumption, by any standards the Social Contract was a success. Its achievements in economic growth, inflation and social progress are impressive. The early period, from 1974 to 1976, up until the moment the aid of the IMF was sought, was especially successful. As it turned out, the prescriptions of the IMF were injurious and imposed very severe strains on the Social Contract itself. But to argue, as the Tories tend to do, that the very conception of the Social Contract led the country to bankruptcy and economic disaster is a grotesque distortion which only Conservative economists with their utter contempt for history would offer" (the text of the lecture is an appendix to Foot, *Another Heart and Other Pulses*, Collins, 1984).

3. Beckett, Ibid, p.489

4. Kathleen Burk, "Money and Power: America and Europe in the 20th Century", *History Today*, Volume 43, 1993.

5. Darrell E. Levi, *Michael Manley: The Making of a Leader*, Andre

Deutsch, 1989, Chapters 15-20.

6. David Renton, *Dissident Marxism*, Zed Books, 2004. The full text of a fascinating chapter on David Widgery, a prime mover and advocate of RAR and the ANL, is here: http://www.dkrenton.co.uk/anl/widgery.html

7. An offshoot of the ANL march to Victoria Park went to Southall to support the picket line at Grunwick, one of the most important industrial disputes of the late 1970s in which low paid Asian women took the initiative in demanding union recognition. The strike attracted much support in other unions, with an NUM contingent turning up one day to turn the tide against a heavily armoured police force. The ANL added to that. But in the rush of class and racial solidarity few stopped to ponder the significance of the final outcome of the Grunwick dispute. The unions lost.

8. Wainwright, Rowbotham & Segal, *Beyond the Fragments*, 1980, Merlin, p.9. *Beyond the Fragments* contains too many insights and political nuggets of gold to summarise fully. The rejection of its arguments by the "hard left" of the time was a tragedy that drove many feminists – though not the authors – towards the lifestyle socialism of *Marxism Today* and its endpoint in Blairism.

9. Pete Goodwin, "Beyond the Fragments", International Socialism 2:9, Summer 1980
http://www.marxists.org/history/etol/newspape/isj2/1980/no2-009/goodwin.html

10. Sassoon, Ibid, p.531

11. Wainwright and Elliott, Ibid, p.114-15

12. A full facsimile of the Ridley Plan including the Confidential Annex can be found at
http://www.margaretthatcher.org/document/110795

13. Naomi Klein, in *The Shock Doctrine* (Penguin, 2007) stripped bare the policies of neo-liberal elites when confronted with exceptional disasters and crises, whether economic or

natural. The leadership of the UK Conservative Party exemplified this approach when constructing an opportunistic governmental coalition with "useful idiots" (the Liberal Democrats) to force an unparalleled programme of social and economic austerity on to the UK after the 2010 General Election, policies on which neither party had stood in the election. The end result has been an unprecedented attempt to return the country to the level of public spending last seen in 1948, which in the opinion of the liberal economist Will Hutton "will do permanent damage to Britain" and will involve "a giant step backwards to a 19th century system of poverty relief" (Hutton, *Observer*, 8th December 2013). For a summary of the threat to UK public services caused by austerity and the policy response of the British trade union movement, on the eve of the TUC "March For the Alternative" on 26th March 2011, see John Medhurst, EPSU/ETUI Conference 23rd February 2011, http://www.epsu.org/IMG/pdf/110223_summary_presentation_John_Medhurst.pdf

14. "Austerity measures spell social catastrophe in Greece", Katarina Selin, 13th August 2011 https://www.wsws.org/en/articles/2011/08/gree-a13.html. See Laurie Penny, *Discordia*, 2012, Kindle edition, for a powerful report from the front line of Greece's agony.

15. *One Million Climate Jobs: Solutions to the Economic and Environmental Crisis,* Report by the Campaign Against Climate Change trade union group in conjunction with CWU, PCS, TSSA and UCU. See also *Unlocking Green Enterprise: A Low-Carbon Strategy for the UK Economy,* TUC Touchstone Pamphlet, for interesting ideas on a transition to a green economy, which because of private sector failure to invest in sustainable solutions would have to be directed and regulated by the public sector.

16. Richard Seymour, "The collapse of the consensus, the myth

of popular capitalism, and the new realism" August 11th 2010,
http://www.leninology.com/2010/08/collapse-of-consensus-myth-of-popular.html

17. In "The Soviet Union versus Socialism", *Our Generation*, Spring/Summer 1986, Noam Chomsky points out that despite the rhetoric of Lenin's *State and Revolution* once they were in power the Bolsheviks moved to contain and then destroy real participatory democracy; "On November 3, Lenin announced in a 'Draft Decree on Workers' Control' that delegates elected to exercise such control were to be 'answerable to the State for the maintenance of the strictest order and discipline and for the protection of property' As the year ended, Lenin noted that 'we passed from workers' control to the creation of the Supreme Council of National Economy,' which was to 'replace, absorb and supersede the machinery of workers' control' (Carr). 'The very idea of socialism is embodied in the concept of workers' control," one Menshevik trade unionist lamented; the Bolshevik leadership expressed the same lament in action, by demolishing the very idea of socialism.'"
http://www.chomsky.info/articles/1986——.htm
See also Emma Goldman and Victor Serge on their experiences in Soviet Russia 1918-21 for how the Bolsheviks crushed workers' control and persecuted anarchists and socialists who advocated it.

18. *City A.M's* Finance correspondent Alistair Hetherington informed his readers on November 5th 2013 that "Slowly but surely the public is turning its back on the market economy and embracing an atavistic version of socialism ...". Referencing surveys which asked people if they supported price controls and the renationalisation of train companies, energy firms and the Royal Mail, he reported that "The results are terrifying" – large majorities supported all these things.

19. In "Egalitarianism in a Global Economy", *Boston Review,* December 1997, the Marxist economist Andrew Glyn stressed the paramount importance of a modern progressive left party creating and sustaining a "coalition of redistribution". For a thought provoking analysis of Glyn's attempts to marry socialist economics with political reality see Stuart White, *The Economics of Andrew Glyn,* in Renewal: A Journal of Social Democracy, www.renewal.org.uk.

20. Sassoon, Ibid, p.697

21. *State Intervention in Industry: A Workers' Inquiry,* Ibid, p.78

22. *The Rubaiyat of Omar Khayyam,* verse 88, translated by Edward Fitzgerald.

Contemporary culture has eliminated both the concept of the public and the figure of the intellectual. Former public spaces – both physical and cultural – are now either derelict or colonized by advertising. A cretinous anti-intellectualism presides, cheerled by expensively educated hacks in the pay of multinational corporations who reassure their bored readers that there is no need to rouse themselves from their interpassive stupor. The informal censorship internalized and propagated by the cultural workers of late capitalism generates a banal conformity that the propaganda chiefs of Stalinism could only ever have dreamt of imposing. Zer0 Books knows that another kind of discourse – intellectual without being academic, popular without being populist – is not only possible: it is already flourishing, in the regions beyond the striplit malls of so-called mass media and the neurotically bureaucratic halls of the academy. Zer0 is committed to the idea of publishing as a making public of the intellectual. It is convinced that in the unthinking, blandly consensual culture in which we live, critical and engaged theoretical reflection is more important than ever before.